The Dismantling of Public Education and How to Stop It

Elaine B. Johnson

ScarecrowEducation
Lanham, Maryland • Toronto • Oxford
2004

Published in the United States of America
by ScarecrowEducation
An imprint of The Rowman & Littlefield Publishing Group, Inc.
4501 Forbes Boulevard, Suite 200, Lanham, Maryland 20706
www.scaroweducation.com

PO Box 317
Oxford
OX2 9RU, UK

British Library Cataloguing in Publication Information Available

Library of Congress Cataloging-in-Publication Data

Johnson, Elaine B.
  The dismantling of public education and how to stop it / Elaine B. Johnson.
    p. cm.
  Includes bibliographical references and index.
  ISBN 1-57886-074-1 (pbk. : alk. paper)
  1. Public schools—United States. 2. Education—Aims and objectives
  United States. 3. Educational change—United States. I. Title.
  LA217.2 .J64 2003
  371.01′0973—dc21

                                                                    2003011920

⊗™ The paper used in this publication meets the minimum requirements of
American National Standard for Information Sciences—Permanence of
Paper for Printed Library Materials, ANSI/NISO Z39.48–1992.
Manufactured in the United States of America.

To the public school teachers who shared their light,
especially Mabel Roberts, and to my family.

Contents

Introduction: The Dismantling of American Education—Are
You for It? ix

1 What Do You Want from Public Schools? 1

2 What Is Business Doing to America's Schools? 21

3 Modern Science—A Guide to Better Schools 53

4 Improving Your Child's Public School 69

5 Good Teaching Connects Lessons with Life: Teaching
History, Science, and Foreign Languages in Context 89

6 Mathematics and Clear Thinking for Everyone 105

Bibliography 125

Index 131

About the Author 137

Acknowledgments

This book reflects the influence of many outstanding teachers and administrators from kindergarten through college. They helped me understand their work and concerns as I visited educational institutions from Anchorage to Orlando and Boston to Anaheim during the past five years. Their longing to help every student achieve high expectations and their urgent sense that something must be done now to strengthen America's one system of public education are reflected in these pages.

I am grateful to Kay Atwood, Dorothy Bennett, Frances Caldwell, Ann Crystal, Ed and Wendy Oliver, Arlene Parisot, Roussel Sargent, and Cathy Yetter for their suggestions and encouragement. I am also grateful to Lorna Spear, the talented principal of Bemiss Elementary School in Spokane, Washington, for so magnanimously explaining the strategies that transformed Bemiss Elementary into an exemplary school. Chapter 4 tells her remarkable story. Chapters 5 and 6 rely heavily on the unpublished work of three exceptional teachers: Todd Duncan, David Gurney, and Judy Reihard. Dr. Todd Duncan, an astrophysicist from the University of Chicago, teacher at Portland State University, and president of the Science Integration Institute, deserves credit for the examples on teaching science. I am also indebted to Todd for his essential help putting scientific concepts in layman's terms. Dr. David Gurney is an associate professor at the University of Central Florida, where he designed the university's certification program in foreign language education and coordinated it until 1998. Well known for his study of how human beings learn new languages, he applies brain research to language acquisition. Many of his insights inform my treatment of foreign language instruction. Judy Reihard, a vocational mathematics specialist in Arizona and a classroom mathematics teacher for over thirty years, has on three occasions received the Award of Excellence honoring her ability to make mathematics accessible to students of all ages and abilities. The mathematics examples and explanations are Judy's. Judy, Todd, and David have given substance to my theories. Their classroom successes show that *every* student can excel when teachers from elementary school through university give lessons meaning by connecting them with the context of student's lives.

Above all I appreciate the generous advice of Peter Senge, author of *The Fifth Discipline* (1990), and the meticulous attention given the manuscript by H. Thomas Johnson, a professor of business and the author of *Profit beyond Measure* (2000). Their suggestions have clarified and strengthened the final text.

Introduction: The Dismantling of American Education—Are You for It?

Education is a matter of intense debate as America moves into the twenty-first century. Businesses use schools to further their own agendas, public interest groups are demanding that schools serve their private goals, teachers are in conflict with principals, and superintendents are pressured by federal mandates to implement policies they dislike. Furthermore, many policy makers, business alliances, and even some educators argue that America's single system of public education must be dismantled and replaced by many autonomous schools competing for customers.[1]

The decisions we make about education have momentous consequences, of course. They touch children's lives today; they shape the kind of person each child will become; and they decide the future of America's democratic society. Most people seem to agree that the primary goal of America's public schools should be to help all young people acquire academic knowledge and develop their unique talents. Given this goal, parents rightly ask, "Does the public school system give my children varied and challenging opportunities to develop their minds? Does it require them to meet high academic standards? Does it draw forth their full promise?"

In addition to helping children develop their full potential, schools have a second important goal. This goal is to instill in young people the deep understanding that they belong to an indivisible humanity. America's racial, ethnic, and economic diversity, coupled with the fact that distant countries have become virtual next-door neighbors, requires that young people learn to respect and appreciate those of various skin hues, races, and cultures. Unless schools help students prize those who are different than they, admire the uniqueness of others, and act responsibly on behalf of their community, fragmentation and discord are inevitable. Do our public schools now teach young people compassionate regard for others? Do they provide a laboratory where young people learn to respect human beings of every race, ethnicity, and economic level, as well as all other species with which they share the planet?

Although many may agree that education should teach young people that they are inextricably linked to all human beings and that education should help students reach high academic standards and nurture their individual talents, there is not general agreement on how to attain these goals. The system of public education that has existed in America for over 150 years is in serious jeopardy. Some believe that America needs to preserve, transform, and revitalize its single system of public education. Others believe that a single system is no longer viable.

Repeated criticisms have greatly eroded popular support for traditional schooling. It is ironic that popular confidence in a single educational system has seriously diminished considering that until the final two decades of the twentieth century, most Americans were proud of their public schools. By 1980 these schools had expanded to absorb millions of children. The United States was providing more schooling to more children than any other nation. By the early 1980s, shortly before the appearance of "A Nation at Risk"—the sensational report on education commissioned during the Reagan administration that assailed public education—about 99 percent of the children eligible to attend elementary school did so, and 71 percent of all seventeen-year-olds graduated from high school. Among high school graduates, 50 percent enrolled in college. By the 1980s, furthermore, schools had done a great deal to stop the abuses of segregation, discrimination against the disabled, and sex discrimination. Schools had also graduated an enormous number of informed young people who became responsible citizens and accomplished scientists, journalists, designers, musicians, engineers, business leaders, and physicians.[2]

It should also be noted that throughout the 1980s and 1990s, state departments of education and school districts plunged enthusiastically into extensive reforms that raised academic standards and improved teaching methods in kindergarten through high school. Their remarkable successes in both academic and vocational programs have been overshadowed, unfortunately, by the barrage of criticism aimed at public education.

Perhaps the most frequent complaint brought against public schools is that academic standards are too low. Alarmed parents fear that their children will receive high school diplomas without learning to read, write, understand science, or solve mathematical problems. Academic quality has deteriorated in part, it is argued, because America's educational system is too bureaucratic. It is too top heavy and too strangled by regulations to provide either quality leadership or excellent instruction. The bureaucratic structure of school districts condemns them to failure.[3] Those who fault the "bureaucratization" of schools see as unwieldy the top-down hierarchical structure of school systems in which teachers report to principals, principals report to superintendents, superintendents report to local school boards, and the entire school district is bound by regulations and rules handed down by policy makers. Such a system, they say, prevents teachers from freely responding to the needs of students. Furthermore, they see such a system as coercive. John E. Chubb and Terry M. Moe, outspoken critics of the traditional public school system, explain that the "bureaucracy problem" refers to the fact that "democratic institutions allocate decision making rights" when they give authority to elected and appointed officials. These officials, winners according to the rules of democracy, are free to set policies that losers have to accept: "In this sense, democracy is essentially coercive."[4]

In addition to objecting to the bureaucratic structure of public education, people also object to the apparent inability of schools to deal with the appalling problems generated by social conditions. Broken families, unemployment, drug abuse, peer pressure, and violence make public schools dangerous places. During the 1990s "more than two hundred shooting deaths occurred in American schools."[5] In the absence of discipline, furthermore, widespread bullying has generated fear and chaos. These practical problems cause many parents to turn away from traditional public schools.[6]

Increasingly convinced that improving traditional schools cannot be done, the general public appears ready to abandon America's single system of public (originally known as "common") education. They seek primarily to replace it with a wide variety of unique public schools—charter schools. Charter schools operate chiefly in isolation from one another, each focused on its own distinctive goals and curriculum. These schools emulate private sector education where "the owners of a school have the legal authority to create whatever kind of school they please, but they cannot require anyone to attend."[7] Like private schools, these distinctive public schools possess autonomy. No rules from above govern them. Like private schools, furthermore, these new kinds of public schools—charter schools—compete in the marketplace for customers. Proponents of this version of public education, although they recognize that "markets are less likely to generate the diversity, quality, and levels of services that customers want," believe that markets should decide whether a public school stays open or closes its doors.[8] Voucher programs and homeschooling are also proposed as viable alternatives to traditional public education.

Is this a good thing? Will our young people and the United States benefit from the transformation of one unified system of public education with common goals into a multitude of schools founded by separate groups, each pursuing its own agenda? Should the traditional single system of public education be dismantled and replaced with some other approach to public education? To answer this question requires examining a number of related, equally important issues. Is it really possible to improve existing public schools—suburban and inner city, urban and rural—so much that they help each student reach high academic standards? What produces quality education anyway? Are specialized public schools—charter schools—the pathway to excellence?

Looking at education from many different angles suggests that the traditional public school system can and should be revitalized, reinvigorated, and preserved as a single system sharing common goals and underlying principles. *Traditional* is used in this book not to refer to worn out teaching methods, a moribund curriculum, or meaningless multiple-choice tests. *Traditional* designates simply the single system of education, the common system, that has always served the public. This single system of public education brings together young people of widely varied races, ethnic groups, economic levels, and social circumstances. It invites them to discover the common humanity that weaves them into a coherent whole. Furthermore, America's single system of education strives to see that all children enjoy the equal opportunity to learn, which is their constitutional right.

It may be that charter schools, liberated from hierarchical constraints, highly innovative, and responsive to their communities, have the potential to become the new single system of public education for the twenty-first century. To do so, these separate schools would have to cultivate interdependence as well as independence by endorsing the same fundamental principles and essential goals. Although generally speaking traditional schools do not have the freedom to innovate that charter schools enjoy, nonetheless, a great many established public schools are highly innovative. Many cases exist of unsatisfactory schools metamorphosing into excellent institutions. These cases suggest that traditional public schools can be reformed, reinvigorated, and revitalized to offer quality education to every child.

Reform and innovation are necessary in part because over time education has evolved to look like business. In effect, education and business have coevolved in response to their twentieth-century context. Like most businesses, our public system of education is hierarchical, cumbersome, and often rigid. As in business, typically school employees are driven by arbitrary, externally imposed targets. As in business, those at the top of the hierarchical structure expect schools to focus on these targets, even if doing so may have damaging repercussions. Like many of today's business leaders, educators often fail to recognize that their organizations are inextricably connected to, and must be responsive to, the surrounding community. As in business, so in education the conviction is strong that people succeed when they work alone and compete. In response to the pressures of their twentieth-century world, education and business alike produce human insecurity, emotional imbalance, stress, ill-health, and hard indifference to the human community, other creatures, and Earth.

It is unlikely that the ills of public education, so similar to those of business, can be remedied by making schools even more like business than they have become. Nevertheless, policy makers and some educators advocate applying to education the business practices set forth in MBA programs. Confidence in business practices has given impetus to the creation of charter schools, voucher programs, and mandatory statewide achievement tests. Because the MBA business model has failed numerous corporations, its effect on education bears careful scrutiny. It is true that local businesses do offer a valuable context in which students can apply academic lessons. They are essential partners in the educational process. However, the basic precepts that direct many small businesses and large corporations do not provide a sound model for designing schools.

Principles derived from modern science do suggest new ways to reinvigorate and redesign public schools. Emerging from modern science are three universal principles—the principles of interrelatedness, self-organization, and differentiation. These principles suffuse and influence everything from subatomic particles to distant galaxies. They permeate and inform all living systems. Living systems survive and flourish because of these universal principles.

Because schools are living systems, it follows that the same principles that enable living systems to adapt, adjust, and thrive apply to schools. Rather than impose abstract, artificial constructs on schools, let school boards, superintendents, principals, teachers, parents, and the community apply nature's principles to existing schools. By nurturing the existing school—the context, the means—according to the principles of modern science, educators, business leaders, and parents will discover new possibilities for creative action and new directions. Applying nature's principles to the organization's context yields the desired results. The end takes care of itself.

Emphasizing the interrelatedness of all things, the universal principles derived from modern science invites us to see the school system as part of, not divorced from, the community. The entire community partners with schools to assure that all students received a quality education. Interaction among parents, teachers, administrators, business leaders, and politicians replaces misunderstanding and fragmentation with encouragement and a coherent sense of purpose.

These conclusions are developed in chapters covering the aims of education, the difficulties with imposing business practices on education, the applicability to education of the principles of modern science, specific methods for leading and improving traditional public schools, and effective strategies for teaching science, mathematics, and foreign languages. Together the following chapters offer a positive picture of quality academic education delivered with an even hand by school districts everywhere for the benefit of children of every race, ethnicity, and economic condition. They also show that America's single system of public education is necessary to unite a diverse population into a democratic society.

NOTES

1. Joel Spring, *The American School: 1642–2000,* 5th ed. (Boston: McGraw Hill, 2000), 428–30.

2. Lawrence A. Cremin, *American Education: The Metropolitan Experience, 1876–1980* (New York: Harper and Row, 1988), 645; Diane Ravitch, *Left Back: A Century of Battles over School Reform* (New York: Simon and Schuster, 2000), 420, 423; Sheila Curran Bernard and Sarah Mondale, *School: The Story of American Public Education,* ed. Sarah Mondale and Sarah B. Patton (Boston: Beacon Press, 2001), 70, 186, 212.

3. David Mathews, *Is There a Public for Public Schools?* (Dayton: Kettering Foundation Press, 1996), 1–26.

4. John E. Chubb and Terry M. Moe, *Politics, Markets, and America's Schools* (Washington, D.C.: Brookings Institution, 1990), 28.

5. Bernard and Mondale, *School,* 210.

6. See Gene Carter, "Watching Out for Our Poorest Schools," available at www.ascd.org/educationnews/kids/kids092002.html (accessed 15 March 2002); see also James D. Anderson, "Introduction" to "Why Don't You Go to School with Us?" in Sheila Curran Bernard and Sarah Mondale, *School: The Story of American Public Education,* ed. Sarah Mondale and Sarah B. Patton (Boston: Beacon Press, 2001), 123–30.

7. Chubb and Moe, *Politics, Markets, and America's Schools,* 29.

8. Chubb and Moe, *Politics, Markets, and America's Schools,* 29.

CHAPTER 1

What Do You Want from Public Schools?

America's free public educational system has had from the beginning both academic and social aims. The primary *academic* aim of education, everyone seems to agree, is to teach subjects such as reading, writing, mathematics, science, literature, and history—and to teach them thoroughly.[1] Even vocational programs, for example, increasingly see their mission as teaching rigorous academic material as well as specific skills. The basic *social* aim of education in the twenty-first century is less apparent. In fact, many question whether schools should have a social aim of any kind.[2] Interest groups, according to noted education historian Lawrence A. Cremin, have over the years sought to use education to teach everything imaginable, from the merits of the capitalist system, Christianity, patriotism, and "the evils of alcohol to dairy products."[3] The Constitutional Rights Foundation wants young people to study how public policy is shaped. Robert J. Sternberg, a professor of psychology and education at Yale University, thinks that schools should teach wisdom.[4] Business groups have advocated that an aim of education should be vocational training to prepare young people for the workplace. This chapter argues that the major *social* aim of public schools must be, as it has been in the past, communicating a common culture. The difficult task is to define that common culture.

In the past, the dominant voice in American society was Protestant. The Protestant majority believed that the proper social aim of education was to unify the nation by teaching a common morality based on Protestant religious beliefs. Today there is no dominant voice. People with nothing in common—not race, country of origin, religion, social customs, simple tastes, or basic values—live shoulder to shoulder in the United States, the most culturally diverse population on earth. Skins in more hues and from more places than ever before in the history of humankind attend the same public schools. Furthermore, Gary Orfield, an expert on desegregation policy, predicts that by the year 2030 most *children* attending school in America will not be white. By 2050 most of the *people* living in America will not be white. Whites will only be one among many minorities. No group will be in the majority.[5] What beliefs and attitudes will this culturally diverse population of minorities share that mold them into a unified democratic society? What commonly held ideas might bring them together? In the twenty-first century, as Harvard University professor Henry Louis Gates Jr. has commented, "the challenge facing America will be the shaping of a truly common public culture."[6]

Given the great diversity of America's people and given that the nation is a democratic society, surely the common cultural idea to be taught in schools is that human beings are inextricably connected. Indeed, perhaps one of the most profound discoveries of modern science is that everything in the universe is connected to everything else in a web of relationships. The climate in the Amazon rain forest can affect the weather in New Jersey. Car-buying habits in Alabama can affect politics in Kuwait. What happens to one part of the web affects the rest of the web. This means that what happens to one person in society concerns everyone. The primary social aim of public education should be to teach this worldview to its diverse student population. Traditional public schools have the potential to instill in young people of every race, ethnicity, and social level the knowledge that every individual is skilled, intelligent, and capable of great deeds. Such understanding begins, of course, when society does what it purports to do—when it gives students equal opportunities to learn.

EQUAL OPPORTUNITY FOR EVERY CHILD?

In the nineteenth century, Americans chose to pay taxes to support a free school system that would bring together children from all levels of society and from many different countries. This tax-supported free school system, which embodied the freedom and equality promised in the Constitution and the Bill of Rights, aimed to give all children the chance to develop their minds and achieve their ambitions. All students would learn, presumably, in the same warm, clean, well-lighted, well-equipped schools where excellent teachers would help them master academic subjects and develop their talents. Public schools would provide an educational ladder sufficient to lift every child to a place of financial security and personal fulfillment.[7]

Everyone realizes, of course, that America's young people have never actually enjoyed equal opportunities to obtain a sound education. Equal opportunity has not really existed in the past, and it still does not exist today. Society neglects some people's children. Society's failure to hold every child in high esteem is rooted in part in racial discrimination as old as the nation itself.

When they wrote the Constitution, George Washington, Benjamin Franklin, Thomas Jefferson, John Adams, James Madison, and other founding fathers decided quite intentionally not to address the problem of slavery. They realized that if the Constitution denounced and outlawed slavery, then it would never receive the support of the southern colonies. Prudence required silence. As a private citizen, Benjamin Franklin was outspokenly opposed to slavery. George Washington deplored slavery and arranged in his will that, upon his death, his slaves should be freed. He also stipulated in his will that Mount Vernon should be sold gradually and piecemeal to provide money to aid the freed slaves. John Adams also decried slavery and was proud never to have owned another human being. Nevertheless, these men and their colleagues bowed to expedience and agreed to support a Constitution that ignores slavery.[8] The problem they felt unable to tackle exploded into the Civil War approximately one generation after the deaths in 1826 of John Adams and Thomas Jefferson. Abraham Lincoln's "Second Inaugural Address," delivered when North and South had been battling for over three years, considers the Civil War to be divine retribution for condoning slavery. Lincoln suggests that God was using the Civil War to punish Southerners and Northerners alike for the enslavement of human beings:

The Almighty has His own purposes. "Woe unto this world because of offenses! It must needs be that offense comes, but woe to that man by whom offence cometh!" . . . American Slavery is one of those offences which, in the providence of God, . . . He now wills to remove, and . . . He gives *to both* North and South this terrific war, as the woe due *to those* by whom the offence came. . . . Fondly do we hope, fervently do we pray that this *mighty scourge* of war may speedily pass away.[9]

The war ended, but the racist mentality that Lincoln and many of his contemporaries denounced lived on.[10] Segregation practiced by local communities in the North and South alike was upheld by the U.S. Supreme Court in 1886 when it ruled that if facilities were equal, then segregation was constitutional. Not until 1954 did the U.S. Supreme Court, in *Brown v. Board of Education,* finally strike down the separate but equal ruling. Even then, segregation continued.[11] Martin Luther King Jr., calling for an end to segregation in the 1960s, reminded audiences that as members of the same human family, "black and white, Eastern and Western, Gentile and Jew, Catholic and Protestant, Moslem and Hindu . . . [all] must learn somehow to live with each other in peace."[12]

Waves of immigration intensified the racial prejudice that had plagued the nation since its inception. In the 1840s and 1850s and from 1880 to 1920, waves of immigrants from all parts of Europe as well as China and Japan came to America. Trapped in an alien place, unable to board a 747 for a quick visit home, without CNN and daily television news, these early immigrants were cut off entirely and seemingly forever from the people and traditions they left behind. Their strategy was, in most cases, to downplay differences that might set them apart from the culture they had joined.

Changes in immigration policies in the late 1960s brought as many immigrants to the United States during the final decades of the twentieth century as had come 100 years earlier. They arrived this time from such distant places as Latvia, Russia, Korea, Guatemala, Trinidad, Malaysia, Peru, Nigeria, Estonia, Laos, and Vietnam. This time, thanks to modern technology, immigrants have maintained connections with their distant homelands and with the relatives and friends they left behind. They have become Americans who do not suppress, but instead proudly celebrate, their cultural identity.[13]

The spectacular diversity of America is a source of robustness and strength. Diversity encourages creativity, innovation, and change. Teaching children to appreciate their classmates because of, not in spite of, their race and ethnicity must be a major social aim of public education. Public schools are capable of nurturing respect for the uniqueness and potential of every human being.

Traditional public schools are positioned to achieve this social goal because they bring together children from a huge variety of ethnicities, races, economic levels, and social conditions. In traditional public schools, students from completely different backgrounds see firsthand that every individual is capable, interesting, and thoughtful. Studying and collaborating together, students find out that every person's well-being is linked inextricably to the well-being of others. Students from widely differing backgrounds learn in traditional public schools that everyone is valuable and that a democratic society exists to benefit everyone, not just a privileged few. Democracy is not about letting the right people have their say. It is about letting everyone have a say. A decision is democratic only if everyone participates in reaching it.[14] As John Dewey has said, emphasizing that a democracy binds people to one another, "A democracy is more than a form of government; it is . . . a mode of associated living, of conjoint, communicated experience. [Therefore] . . . each has to refer his own action to that of others and to consider the actions of others" in breaking down "barriers of class, race, and national territory."[15] All races and cultures in the United States can bridge the chasm caused by different religious beliefs, experiences, and customs. Traditional public schools can help young people learn to appreciate and nurture a unified society with truly equal opportunity for all. They can teach children that living together cooperatively, not competitively, all races and cultures in the United States can together sustain a unified, free, and just society.

Unfortunately, the trend among many people today seems to be to look for those who are like themselves. Rather than thank those whose distinctive customs, beliefs, and tastes enrich their lives, people shun them. They do not welcome differences as opportunities to enlarge their thinking. Instead, they turn away from minorities, the disabled, the poor, and people whose religions are different from their own. Forgetting that sameness limits the mind and shrinks the spirit, parents send their children to special schools—charter schools and private schools—where students tend to resemble one another. The proliferation of these schools may pose obstacles for the hard-won desegregation achieved in school districts throughout the country. How can America's immensely diverse children develop a common culture and share a common vision if, isolated in their specialized public and private schools, they do not interact and learn together?

VOUCHERS TO THE RESCUE?

Many public officials and parents see in the voucher system a way to obtain equal educational opportunities for America's children. Under this system the government gives money to students in the form of vouchers, and students use these vouchers to pay tuition at the secular or religious schools of their choice. The U.S. Supreme Court upheld the use of vouchers in 2002 with its five-four ruling that taxpayer money could be used to send children to private or parochial schools.[16] Defending this ruling, Chief Justice William Rehnquist argued that because the voucher program gives families "true private choice," it does not break the barrier between church and state. He also held that vouchers would make it possible for children of low-income families to obtain a quality education at excellent private schools.[17]

Speaking against the use of vouchers, U.S. Supreme Court Justice David Souter argued that a voucher system violates the core constitutional principle that the government shall not financially support religious instruction. Justice Souter's position echoes the 1947 decision of Supreme Court Justice Hugo Black that "no tax, in any amount, large or small, can be levied to support any religious activities or institutions, whatever they may be called, or whatever form they may adopt to teach or practice religion."[18]

While Justice Souter and others oppose the voucher system on the grounds that it breaks down the separation of church and state, many people also oppose the voucher system on the grounds that it threatens the existence of America's traditional single public school system. Vouchers endanger public education by giving young people taxpayer dollars to *leave* public schools, in the process draining financial support away from public schools.

Ironically, this drain subsidizes secular and religious schooling primarily for children of the affluent, not for the children of low-income families. Three-quarters of all students who accept vouchers to pay tuition at private schools are already attending such schools.[19] Families that are already sending their children to private schools are delighted to accept from taxpayers a voucher that reduces by about $2,500 their personal investment in a tuition bill that might exceed $6,000 per year.

Because most vouchers are worth $2,500 or less, the value of a voucher is not sufficient to cover tuition at an outstanding private school.[20] For the most part, in fact, low-income children find that their vouchers will cover tuition only at relatively inexpensive inner-city Catholic schools that may for good reason have empty seats. The voucher system does not give low-income children, as it is purported to do, a quality private education.

The cost of tuition is not the only factor that keeps the children of low-income families out of secular and parochial schools. These private schools are under no obligation to accept vouchers from poor students. They can bar all but the *right* clients. Even admission to mediocre private schools is far from certain. Private schools, as everyone knows, sort young people and exclude those who do not measure up. Parents should be troubled that this sorting is now financed by tax dollars, taxes intended originally to pay for a democratic system of education that guarantees equal opportunities to all children. It is disturbing that voucher programs drain public money from public schools to make it available for use at private schools when these private schools screen the young applicants holding vouchers. Of course, in their quest for desirable students, private schools may exclude applicants for virtually any reason.

Adherents of the voucher system praise it for rescuing the poor and minorities from ineffectual schools, but it does not rescue them. It leaves them behind. The voucher system fails to fulfill the academic aim of providing a quality education that helps all students meet high academic standards.

It also fails the social aim of teaching young people to live in harmony as members of a common culture. Rather than give children the chance to interact and learn with fellow students from different ethnicities, races, and economic backgrounds, the voucher system itself sorts and separates. Unfortunately, when children leave traditional public schools to walk a private path, they are in danger of looking only for sameness and of dismissing the wonderful diversity that is the fabric of a democratic society.

WHOSE RELIGION?

Far more troubling and volatile than the voucher system is the question of religion in public schools. Many parents consider the failure of public schools to teach religion as a compelling reason to take their children out of traditional public schools. Parental discontent poses the issue, "Should religious education be a social aim of public education? Does religion have a place in the curriculum from kindergarten through high school?"

Since the nineteenth century it has been widely held that public schools should teach Protestant Christianity to America's youth. In the mid-nineteenth century, Horace Mann, the driving force behind free public (then known as "common") education, urged that Christian values be incorporated into the school day to promote good character and civic virtue. Like Mann, Protestant evangelicals and fundamentalists also sought to produce virtuous citizens by incorporating Protestant beliefs into public education. For example, evangelists in Ohio, Michigan, and throughout the Midwest established common public schools that featured Protestant hymns, the King James Version of the Bible, and prayer.[21] At the time, many considered such religious instruction to be an excellent way to shape young people into right-thinking members of a coherent nation. From its inception, however, the Protestant tone of America's public schools was a source of great discontent.

Roman Catholics regarded the dominant Protestant voice as intolerable. To escape the Protestant tone of public schools, they founded their own parochial schools: "In 1900 there were about 900,000 pupils in Catholic schools, and by 1963 there were 5.5 million, or 14 percent of the total school age population."[22] James W. Fraser, a professor of history and education at Northeastern University, shows how harrowing it is to be made to participate in someone else's religion by citing the Austrian Judaic scholar Martin Buber. Buber says of his own experience at school, "The obligatory daily standing in the room resounding with the strange service affected me worse than an act of intolerance could have affected me. . . . [It] stamped itself upon the life-substance of the boy."[23]

Over the years, the complexion of America gradually changed, and citizens began to object with increasing force and energy to the mingling of church and state. In *Engle v. Vitale* (1962) and *Abington v. Schempp* (1963), the U.S. Supreme Court denied, respectively, the official use of prayer and Bible reading in schools. With these rulings, the Protestant ascendancy in schools ended.[24] Opponents of Bible reading and prayer in schools based their objections on the Constitution's guarantee of freedom from coercion in matters of faith.

That freedom began, interestingly, as a protective measure. Fraser points out in his excellent book, *Between Church and State: Religion and Public Education in a Multicultural America,* that all of the delegates to the Continental Congress, such as the Congregationalists from Massachusetts and the Anglicans from Virginia, subscribed to the religious beliefs peculiar to their home regions. Confident that its colony's way of worshiping was the right way, each delegation—had it the votes to do so—would gladly have compelled other regions to adopt its colony's religious beliefs and practices. But the delegations did not have the votes, and they did not want to be coerced themselves to adopt some other colony's religion. Out of self-interest, therefore, the delegates supported the separation of church and state. Separating church and state was an expedient act intended to preserve each colony's religious freedom. As Fraser puts it, "Everyone wanted religious freedom for themselves, and the only way they saw to get it was to grant it, however, grudgingly, to others."[25]

When the Continental Congress declared the separation of church and state, thus guaranteeing the right to worship according to conscience, it was taking a radical stand. For over 1,500 years, governments all over the world had strictly controlled religious faith and worship, regarding the church as an arm of government. Today, the separation of church and state is no longer considered, of course, to be radical. On the contrary, around the world, religious freedom is venerated as one of humankind's most fundamental rights.[26]

This right is violated, of course, any time that one religious group compels another to practice its rites or accept its beliefs. Viewed from this perspective, the dissemination in public schools of Protestant beliefs that went on for generations was a form of compulsion, and as such it constituted ideological tyranny. Writing twenty-three years apart, two U.S. Supreme Court justices explain that the tyranny of religious coercion cannot cohabit with democratic governance. Justice William O. Douglas warned in 1966 that passing laws to allow one group to impose its religion on others opens the door for other groups to compel submission to their beliefs. Exaggerating to make a point, Douglas said, "In time Moslems will control some of our school boards. In time devout Moslems may want their prayer in our schools; and if Protestant sects can get their prayers past the barriers of the First Amendment, the same passage would be guaranteed for Moslems."[27] Douglas was clear that no religious group has the right in a democracy to dictate how children shall worship. Religion and morality must remain private and personal. And U.S. Supreme Court Justice Robert Jackson, writing in 1943, anticipated Douglas when he warned that any form of coercion leads to tyranny: "Those who begin coercive elimination of dissent soon find themselves exterminating dissenters. Compulsory unification of opinion achieves only the unanimity of the graveyard. . . . When any ideology is forced on a school, then those who support it seek control of the educational system. Or they weaken the influence of the educational system by fighting with it."[28]

Now that schools have no legal right to require obligatory prayers and Bible reading, dissatisfaction with public education is growing, most notably among the Religious Right. Religious conservatives propose amending the Constitution to return prayer to the schools. They see charter schools and voucher programs as necessary alternatives to a traditional system of education that excludes religious practices.[29] How should twenty-first-century educators think about religion?

Some new ways to think about religion and public education are found in an unexpected place—in the universal principles of interrelatedness, self-organization, and differentiation discovered by modern science. The principle of interrelatedness affirms that all human beings are bound to one another and to all living and nonliving systems. The principle of self-organization holds that any living system changes, adapts, and develops in response to its surroundings. The scientific principle of differentiation describes the creative drive everywhere in the universe toward infinite variety. Taken together, these three principles remind us that human beings are united and that one of the major things uniting them is their drive to create meaning. The quest for spiritual meaning, a fundamental human impulse, is manifest in the world's religions. Thus academic classes that explore all religions—that teach, for instance, Catholic, Protestant, Sikh, Buddhist, Muslim, Hindu, Fundamentalist Christian, and Jewish beliefs—will offer insights into the meaning of human life that students might otherwise miss. Classes on the world's religions also encourage students to understand and respect, never to belittle, dismiss, or trivialize, another person's religious faith.

Many parents see slight merit, if any; however, in a public school system that treats world religions as an academic subject. How, parents ask, will our children benefit from knowing about many religions if they do not believe in any one religion? Is it more important for our children to know about the world's different religions than it is to acquire the family's religious beliefs? Persuaded that transmitting their own faith to their children is of paramount importance, many parents choose schools that will teach children the religion they hold themselves. Removing their children from traditional public schools, they place them instead in parochial or special public schools, charter schools, with a curriculum that complements their religion. Or they use vouchers—"passes"—worth a stated amount of money to pay for their children's tuition at a parochial school.

Is it possible that young people who are exposed only to one religion in twenty-first-century America might have trouble understanding and valuing the culturally and racially diverse people walking side by side in today's global society? Is it possible that they might be deprived of ways of thinking and seeing that might enrich their own lives and increase their ability to enrich the lives of others? Perhaps one of the major social aims of twenty-first-century America's schools should be to expose young people to unfamiliar religious customs and beliefs and in so doing to prepare them to live in a very small, yet fabulously diverse world. Certainly if human beings do not learn to live together in a spirit of tolerance, then twenty-first-century society—a society of minorities—will become increasingly turbulent, contentious, and fragmented, not democratic.

EQUAL OPPORTUNITY FOR ALL AND VOCATIONAL EDUCATION

Just as religious instruction has long been a social aim of public education, and just as we are struggling to understand its place in the twenty-first century, so vocational instruction has for over ninety years been an educational goal, and today we are trying to understand its role in public education. Whether focusing on the abstract domain of spiritual beliefs or the concrete world of job training, we are dealing with highly charged issues that have significant implications for the future of education.

Vocational Education, 1880–1917

Business has never hesitated to shape the aims of education to serve its immediate interests. From approximately 1880 to 1917, and from 1980 to the present day, business groups have pressured public schools to respond to their particular needs. Fulfilling the needs of business, however, has not always served the best interests of students. For decades, in fact, business was largely responsible for depriving thousands of young people of the chance to study academic subjects. Between 1880 and 1917, American companies were having trouble competing with Germany and Great Britain. They blamed their problems in part on a poorly educated workforce. If only high schools did a better job of preparing students for the workplace, business groups contended, then companies could do a better job of competing. Company leaders believed that teaching such practical skills as drafting and welding would strengthen America's industries. With this practical aim in mind, business lobbied hard for high school vocational programs designed to train youths for the workplace. Many influential educators agreed with business leaders that high schools should offer job training. Business lobbying, with strong support from influential professional educators, secured federal subsidies in 1917 that added job training to the academic curriculum in high schools across the nation.[30]

The 1918 report of the National Education Association Commission on the Reorganization of Secondary Education supports making job training a function of high schools. The report contends that many young people do not need to know academic subjects and that others are incapable of learning them. Students who are not smart enough to benefit from studying academic subjects are suited, the report holds, for vocational programs that prepare them for the labor market: Let them take practical classes such as plumbing, cooking, and carpentry; these classes are sufficient.[31] After all, "does a bricklayer really need to know Shakespeare?"[32] Do women really need to know history and science? In the 1920s, a professor at Kansas State Agricultural College expressed the prevailing opinion when he said, "Where does the trigonometry apply in a good woman's life? Will it contribute anything toward peace, happiness and contentment at home? Will it bake any bread? . . . But the girl who has been taught just how to make a dollar do a dollar's worth of service . . . has much permanent culture."[33] He argued, in effect, that if a woman studies only home economics, then she learns enough to keep her husband content, and that is all she needs to know.

Such thinking coincided with the development of the IQ test. At approximately the same time that the federal government agreed to subsidize high school vocational courses, IQ tests were being used in World War I to sort soldiers into officers and infantry. Before long, professional educators and psychologists began to give IQ tests to children. They were convinced that an IQ test could quantify a child's mental aptitude and thus accurately predict the likelihood of that child's academic success. IQ test scores were construed—mistakenly, as we realize today—as hard evidence of intellectual aptitude. Furthermore, when Native Americans, Afro-Americans, Italians, Mexicans, and other minorities scored poorly on IQ tests, blatant prejudice against their cultures fed the conclusion that these young people lacked the inherent ability to grasp challenging academic material.[34]

However, the immigrant children flocking to school at the time, and their parents, knew that only an academic education would lift them out of the slums. Although these students wanted the opportunity to study academic subjects, often they were compelled to take vocational and other nonacademic classes. They were *tracked* into them.

Tracking is an arbitrary sorting procedure that deprives young people of equal opportunities to learn. It places a student in a vocational program on the grounds that he or she *belongs* there and will most assuredly benefit from being there. Tracking is the practice of relegating young people to vocational classes whether they like it or not. Parents may object to seeing their child tracked, ordered to enroll in a carpentry program, when their dream is that he or she should become an electrical engineer. But the sorting system ignores their protestations. Their child will be trained to do construction work.

Fortunately, today people reject tracking as morally reprehensible and realize that IQ tests are unreliable. Brain research has demonstrated that intelligence is far too complex to be quantified. It is not a single, fixed entity that can be measured.[35] That we now understand the fallibility of IQ testing is no solace, of course, to the thousands of young people who were forced to enroll in vocational programs. Equality of opportunity did not exist for them, and their full potential went undiscovered.

Vocational Education, 1980–Present: An Academic Opportunity

It is true that from the early years of the twentieth century until quite recently, tracking arbitrarily sent many students into narrow vocational programs that offered nothing more than training to perform specific tasks for particular occupations. Things are different now. Since the 1980s, vocational education has undergone a stunning transformation. Tracking has virtually disappeared, and academic rigor has arrived. Today vocational and technical programs teach young people to read, write, communicate orally, make multimedia presentations, listen well, compute, and think critically. Students enroll in these programs not because they are shunted into vocational courses but because they choose to take them. In these courses they learn not only practical skills but also academic material.

Incorporating rigorous academic subjects into vocational and technical programs began in the early 1980s. Faced with a new age of technology, an age of endless complexity and constant change, vocational-technical faculty realized that depriving their students of academic knowledge would handicap them for life. Consequently, for over twenty years vocational-technical instructors have been developing, often in collaboration with academic colleagues, highly innovative teaching methods that help all students reach high academic standards. In fact, students who have trouble learning in traditional classrooms often discover that vocational courses, because they involve dealing with subjects in concrete ways, help them grasp difficult academic material. For example, a material sciences high school instructor so successfully uses hands-on methods to teach chemistry that Advanced Placement (AP) chemistry students take his vocational class to better understand their AP course. Because vocational classes apply academic content in a real-world context, students are able to grasp academic lessons that elude them when they are presented abstractly.[36]

Surprisingly, business groups and policy makers do not seem to realize that vocational-technical education no longer resembles the narrow job training introduced with the opening of the first public manual training school in Baltimore in 1884 and extending until about 1980.[37] Today high schools and community colleges in virtually every state have designed vocational-technical programs to contain rigorous academic content. Because these programs teach in a multitude of ways designed to reach widely diverse talents and learning styles, they have become popular. Students realize that in the process of studying, say, computer-aided drafting, graphic design, manufacturing technology, hospitality and tourism, or plumbing, they will also be able to learn composition, critical thinking, mathematics, and science. When students connect academic subjects to their vocational classes, they see meaning in them and are therefore able to master them.

It is ironic that business leaders are willing today to allow vocational programs to die away. Business leaders have the temerity not only to assign to schools the social aim of strengthening America's economic performance in foreign markets but also to presume to tell educators how to achieve this goal. In the early 1900s industry and business insisted that vocational education in high schools was the only educational strategy that would make business competitive. Today, however, they argue that schools will achieve the aim of making business competitive in foreign markets only by supplanting vocational education with traditional academic classes. The fact that young people acquire knowledge in infinitely varied ways, and that some learn academic material best by working in a real-world situation, does not seem to occur to business leaders. They decree aims and impose methods without understanding, apparently, the complex and intricate work of classroom instruction.[38]

Equal Opportunity through Vocational-Technical Education

As we have seen, high schools began offering vocational programs because business needed to increase its competitiveness. Throughout most of the twentieth century, IQ tests tracked young people into vocational classes. Racial prejudice fed the nation's willingness to believe that IQ scores correctly identify ability. It also fed the nation's willingness to deprive thousands of young people of the opportunity to learn academic subjects. Today, however, vocational-technical education is all about opening doors. In addition to giving students specific skills, it helps them master academic subjects. In other words, it prepares them simultaneously to enter the job market, attend a community college, or enter a university.

Because equality of opportunity, not tracking, characterizes today's vocational-technical programs, and because they provide academic knowledge as well as skills, they fulfill an important aim of education. Should Carl Perkins funding, the major source of federal funding for high school vocational programs, be terminated, those who learn by actively connecting academic lessons with the context of practical experience will suffer. Equality of opportunity to learn academic subjects will no longer be theirs.

THE ESSENTIAL SOCIAL AIM: UNDERSTANDING HUMANITY'S COMMON CULTURE

Kofi Annan, the secretary-general of the United Nations, said in his 2001 Nobel Peace Prize acceptance speech that "humanity is indivisible."[39] This truth has the power to unite America's hugely diverse races and ethnicities into a common culture. The indivisibility of humankind is affirmed by modern science, which tells us that everything in the entire universe is related to everything else. It is implicit in the democratic political principle of equality that affirms every person's significance and worth. The child growing up in the slums of South Chicago is as valuable as the child in Mill Valley, California, and deserves identical educational opportunities. The indivisibility of human beings is also apparent in the universal human quest for spiritual insight that manifests itself in the world's religions. Furthermore, the longing of people everywhere to enjoy freedom and peace testifies that humanity is indivisible. The paramount social aim of traditional public education must be to communicate this truth to America's young people. To be fully human, young people must acquire more in school than academic information. They must also acquire the deep knowledge that, as human beings, they are inextricably linked to, and are responsible for, one another and the Earth itself.

NOTES

1. Diane Ravitch, *Left Back: A Century of Battles over School Reform* (New York: Simon and Schuster, 2000), 465; Alfred North Whitehead, "The Aims of Education," in *Aims of Education and Other Essays* (New York: Macmillan, 1929), 2–4.

2. Joel Spring, *The American School: 1642–2000,* 5th ed. (Boston: McGraw Hill, 2000), 118–19.

3. Lawrence A. Cremin, *American Education: The Metropolitan Experience, 1876–1980* (New York: Harper and Row, 1988), 650–51.

4. Robert J. Sternberg, "Teaching for Wisdom in Our Schools," *Education Week on the Web,* 13 November 2002, available at http://ew/ewstory.cfm?slug=//Sternberg.h22#author (accessed 15 November 2002).

5. Sheila Curran Bernard and Sarah Mondale, *School: The Story of American Public Education,* ed. Sarah Mondale and Sarah B. Patton (Boston: Beacon Press, 2001), 167–68.

6. Ravitch, *Left Back,* 425.

7. Carl F. Kaestle, "Introduction" to "The Educated Citizen," in Sheila Curran Bernard and Sarah Mondale, *School: The Story of American Public Education,* ed. Sarah Mondale and Sarah B. Patton (Boston: Beacon Press, 2001), 11; Diane Ravitch, "Introduction" to "You Are an American," in Sheila Curran Bernard and Sarah Mondale, *School: The Story of American Public Education,* ed. Sarah Mondale and Sarah B. Patton (Boston: Beacon Press, 2001), 64.

8. Joseph Ellis, *Founding Brothers: The Revolutionary Generation* (New York: Vintage Books, 2000), 90–94, 115, 158.

9. Abraham Lincoln, "Second Inaugural Address" (facsimile, Historical Documents Co., 1865); Garry Wills, "Lincoln's Greatest Speech?" *Atlantic Monthly,* September 1999: 69.

10. Bernard and Mondale, *School,* 33, 42–44.

11. James W. Fraser, *Between Church and State: Religion and Public*

Education in a Multicultural America (New York: St. Martin's/Griffin, 1999), 79, 150, 201; Bernard and Mondale, *School*, 137–38.

12. Martin Luther King Jr., "Where Do We Go from Here: Chaos or Community?" (1976), in *A Testament of Hope: The Essential Writing and Speeches of Martin Luther King, Jr.*, ed. James M. Washington (San Francisco: Harper-Collins, 1986), 555–633.

13. Spring, *The American School*, 406–07.

14. Louis Menand, *The Metaphysical Club: A Story of Ideas in America* (New York: Farrar, Straus and Giroux, 2001), 432.

15. John Dewey, cited in Cremin, *American Education*, 172.

16. June Kronholz and Robert S. Greenberger, "Supreme Court Ruling Gives Boost to Proponents of School Vouchers," *The Wall Street Journal*, 28 June 2002: A1, A4.

17. David G. Savage, "Court Upholds School Vouchers," *The Oregonian*, 28 June 2002: A1.

18. Savage, "Court Upholds School Vouchers," A15.

19. Bernard and Mondale, *School*, 198; Kronholz and Greenberger, "Supreme Court Ruling Gives Boost to Proponents of School Vouchers," A4.

20. Bernard and Mondale, *School*, 194.

21. David Tyack, "Introduction," in Sheila Curran Bernard and Sarah Mondale, *School: The Story of American Public Education*, ed. Sarah Mondale and Sarah B. Patton (Boston: Beacon Press, 2001), 5; Bernard and Mondale, *School*, 31–33; Fraser, *Between Church and State*, 39.

22. Fraser, *Between Church and State*, 65.

23. Martin Buber, cited in Fraser, *Between Church and State*, 220.

24. Spring, *The American School*, 419–20; Fraser, *Between Church and State*, 146.

25. Fraser, *Between Church and State*, 17.

26. Fraser, *Between Church and State*, 20.

27. William O. Douglas, *The Bible and the Schools* (Boston: Little, Brown, 1966), 45.

28. Robert Jackson, cited in Fraser, *Between Church and State*, 136.

29. Spring, *The American School*, 420.

30. Ravitch, *Left Back*, 37, 459; Spring, *The American School*, 6, 266, 296; Bernard and Mondale, *School*, 175.

31. Ravitch, *Left Back*, 43–44, 124.

32. Joel Spring, cited in Bernard and Mondale, *School*, 99.

33. Cited in Ravitch, *Left Back*, 99–100.

34. Ravitch, *Left Back*, 37, 130–62, 459.

35. Howard Gardner, *The Frames of Mind: The Theory of Multiple Intelligences,* 10th ed. (New York: HarperCollins, 1993), 3–58; Susan Greenfield, *The Human Brain: A Guided Tour* (New York: HarperCollins, 1997), 67–78.

36. Elaine B. Johnson, *Contextual Teaching and Learning: What It Is and Why It's Here to Stay* (Thousand Oaks, Calif.: Corwin Press, Inc., 2002), 1–33.

37. Ravitch, *Left Back,* 37.

38. Larry Cuban, "Introduction" to "A Nation at Risk?" in Sheila Curran Bernard and Sarah Mondale, *School: The Story of American Public Education,* ed. Sarah Mondale and Sarah B. Patton (Boston: Beacon Press, 2001), 174–76.

39. Kofi Annan, "Nobel Lecture December 10, 2001," *Timeline,* no. 63. (May–June 2002): 6–9.

CHAPTER 2

What Is Business Doing to America's Schools?

Most people agree that only if America's school system is reformed will it achieve the aims of education. The nature of this reform is a matter of intense debate. As we enter the twenty-first century, the prevailing voice is that of business leaders and public officials. Stanford education professor Larry Cuban explains that influential corporate leaders and policy makers think that "schools should be modeled after the corporation and the marketplace."[1] Largely at the persistent urging of business roundtables—political action groups consisting of corporate executives and policy makers—"the values, language, organization, and governance of corporate leaders . . . [are being] applied . . . to schools."[2] Because business leaders and public officials have convinced many educators and parents to embrace this "wholesale application of a business model" to education, the "corporate model of market competition, choice, and accountability has been largely copied by districts and states and has spread swiftly."[3]

Should a business model be applied to public schools? Will schools improve student performance if they adopt business practices? Is it possible that following a business model might do more harm than good? This worry is legitimate, considering that business practices do not always serve *business* well. Companies fall into bankruptcy, lay off thousands of workers, demolish retirement funds, prematurely terminate full-time workers to replace them with cheaper part-time labor, demean employees with incentive and penalty programs, pit workers against one another, engage in hostile takeovers, wantonly consume natural resources, and spit out toxic waste that pollutes drinking water and the air we breathe. Business pays top administrators outrageously high salaries, and it tolerates corrupt behavior on the part of top executives, behavior made public only when a company implodes, as did Enron, or when a courageous employee speaks up. In the name of profit, business repeatedly refuses to do the right thing by employees, communities, and the ecosystem.

Given the many shortcomings of business, for what reasons do we assume that following a business model will benefit public education? Is business wise enough to improve America's school system? The answer to this question requires looking at business practices to understand the model they offer schools. The answer also requires looking at charter schools, voucher programs, and standardized achievement tests, the results of education imitating business that affect the fabric of society.

THE THREE COMMANDMENTS OF BUSINESS

The corporate model for business consists of three fundamental commandments: grow, compete, and pursue measurable targets for which employees are held accountable.[4] Are these commandments actually good for companies, or would companies be better off following different practices? If these practices are *not* good for business, then how can they possibly benefit education?

The First Commandment of Business: Grow

MBA students trained since the 1950s have been taught that to be profitable, a corporation must constantly grow. Standard doctrine in MBA programs holds that bigger scale and faster processes will cut costs and increase profits. However, efforts to achieve speed and economies of scale almost invariably result in faulty products, missed deliveries, employee discontent, and customer dissatisfaction. These serious problems are typically dismissed by companies as the regrettable but inevitable side effects of doing business.[5] Because CEOs and CFOs consider growth a necessary source of profit, acquisitions and mergers have become commonplace. Yet growth achieved by these means cannot be counted on to maintain the long-term prosperity of companies, to benefit employees, or to strengthen communities. AOL, Random House, Scott Paper, Chrysler, Asea, Saab, and Time-Warner are just a few of the many companies whose capabilities have been diminished by takeovers and mergers carried out in pursuit of unlimited growth.[6]

The Second Commandment of Business: Compete

That competition is good is a fundamental axiom of business. Companies that compete with formidable opponents in a free market, MBA programs explain, will learn to perform efficiently and effectively. Competing will drive them to satisfy customer needs and to survive over the long haul. The benefits of competition, advocates of free market competition say, are exemplified by the deregulation of airlines. They say that deregulation has resulted in better, cheaper airline service for customers. Opponents of free market competition point out that the deregulation of airlines has adversely affected customers. Airlines have taken advantage of deregulation, opponents claim, to initiate cost-cutting measures that deprive passengers of convenient routes, safe air in cabins, sanitary and toxin-free drinking water, adequate leg room, and edible food. Interestingly, those who support free market competition acknowledge that markets are imperfect. The market's benefits are skewed toward those with the best information and the most resources: "Consumers may be too poorly informed to make choices that are truly in their best interests. . . . The unequal distribution of incomes in society may bias certain markets in favor of the rich and against the poor."[7]

Business confidence in unrestrained market competition arises in part from a misapplication of the principle of natural selection. Business has borrowed the idea of natural selection from the evolutionary theory of "survival of the fittest," which Herbert Spencer introduced seven years before the publication of Darwin's *On the Origin of Species*. Business has long used this theory pertaining to biological species to justify brutal competition. However, to view market competition as the mode of human behavior required for *natural* success is to misrepresent the way human beings naturally relate to one another.[8] In fact, they *naturally* have the capacity to be kind, self-sacrificing, and compassionate. As the first American sociology textbook, *Dynamic So-*

ciology, says, "The survival of the fittest is simply the survival of the strong, which . . . might as well be called the destruction of the weak. And if nature progresses through the destruction of the weak, man progresses through the *protection* of the weak."[9]

Surely the unique capacity of human beings to think, formulate moral values, and benefit from accumulated wisdom borne of long experience challenges the claim that unrestrained competition is good for business. W. Edwards Deming observes in *The New Economics,* "We must throw overboard the idea that competition is a necessary way of life. In place of competition we need cooperation."[10] Deming explains, "If economists understood the theory of a system, and the role of cooperation in optimization, they would no longer teach and preach salvation through adversarial competition. They would, instead, lead us into the best plan for a system, in which everybody would come out ahead."[11] The soundness of Deming's view has been confirmed by his own successes working with companies as well as by the findings of modern science. Indeed, "the pretty dream of a perfect, natural order of things brought about by the free play of unrestrained . . . forces" is only a dream, not science.[12] An economic world committed to unbridled competition, as global business demonstrates, may build, but it also destroys. Relentless competition is not an unequivocally sound practice for business. It is assuredly a dangerous practice for education.

The Third Commandment of Business: Set Measurable Targets and Stress Accountability

With very few notable exceptions, such as the Toyota Motor Corporation and Southwest Airlines, businesses manage by results. To manage by results is to use quantitative targets to drive operations for the entire organization and for subsystems within the organization. Set by top executives on the basis of abstract quantitative information, these targets do not emerge from a deep understanding of a company's day-to-day activities. Distant from the day-to-day work of the companies they control, CEOs and CFOs use accounting numbers as the basis for setting measurable targets to be met by employees. Middle managers in target-driven corporations end up paying more attention to these abstract targets than to the real work carried out by frontline employees.

Removed from the daily operations of the companies they direct, CEOs and CFOs tend not to understand their companies' work. Making management decisions exclusively on the basis of quantitative information, they ignore the complex relationships within each organization.

These relationships, however, actually dictate a company's ultimate financial results. Relationships are of paramount importance because human organizations are living systems, and in any system it is the *interaction* of separate parts that gives life and uniqueness to the whole. Quantitative measures do not divulge how individuals within an organization connect and relate to one another, making possible a company's robustness and profitability. The imperative to meet measurable targets, rather than facilitate work, interferes with the smooth running of an organization. Its disruption threatens success.

The commandment to meet measurable targets is so ingrained in the culture of the business world that those who fail to reach them are punished and those who attain them are rewarded. Employees who meet targets may be made "employee of the month" or given a bonus. Those who fail to meet targets, even when the targets are unrealistic, may be demoted or even fired. Jack Welch, the retired CEO of General Electric, for instance, has made it common knowledge that he required managers to terminate employees who ranked for a stated time in the bottom 10 percent of their respective groups.

Governed by rewards and punishments imposed from above, employees feel controlled and manipulated. They also feel compelled to suppress any recommendations they might be able to make about streamlining the operations they perform. All that matters to their supervisors, after all, is that they meet the target: "If management sets the targets and makes people's jobs depend on meeting them, people will do whatever is needed to hit the targets, including destroying the company to get there."[13]

USING A BUSINESS MODEL HARMS PUBLIC SCHOOLS

The business commandments to grow, compete, set targets, and hold employees accountable for reaching targets do not always serve business well. Do they benefit education, or is their influence damaging to children attending public schools? From these tenets to grow, compete, reach targets, and demonstrate accountability, education has gained big schools, charter schools, and high-stakes standardized achievement tests. Are these practices good for our children and for the nation? Do they improve teaching and learning? Do they achieve the educational aim of academic excellence and the social aim of creating a common culture based on mutual respect? If imitating business does not cause schools to achieve these goals, then education needs to look elsewhere for a model on which to base reform.

THE BUSINESS COMMANDMENT TO GROW HARMS STUDENTS

Business alleges that growth causes efficiency and cuts costs. But when applied to education, the commandment to grow has not contained costs, and students have suffered. Most U.S. public schools were small until the 1950s. During the 1950s and 1960s, business groups, politicians, and educators argued vigorously that large schools "can take advantage of economies of scale in such things as capital investments and administrative costs and thereby operate efficiently."[14] James B. Conant, a president of Harvard University, argues in his influential book, *The American High School* (1959), that small high schools are a financial liability and should be consolidated into large high schools holding up to 2,000 students. In keeping with Conant's advice, between the end of World War II to 1990, 101,000 school districts were consolidated into 15,000. By 1999 only "90,000 U.S. public schools served about 47 million students" in comparison to the case during the 1930s, when "262,000 U.S. public schools served 26 million students."[15] The business practice of economies of scale has so influenced education that by "1996, nearly half of all American high school students attended a high school with an enrollment of more than 1,500 students."[16]

These large schools were praised for being efficient and economical. They were extolled for accommodating youths of all abilities and for providing a rich and varied selection of academic and vocational classes. They were applauded for reducing administrative overhead, capital investments, and operating costs. However, recent studies seriously challenge the claim that big schools are more cost-effective to run, cheaper to build, and cheaper to maintain than small schools.[17]

Even if large schools are cost-effective, are they defensible? Should cost-effectiveness be a primary reason for deciding how we organize schools? Today 70 percent of our youths attend high schools enrolling more than 1,000 students.[18] How are young people affected by attending these immense, impersonal schools? Sending students to massive high schools is tantamount to abandoning them. At a time in their lives when students most need the example of mature, stable adults, adolescents are sent to huge, intimidating schools where loneliness drives them to form destructive alliances with peer groups. Large schools are not communities where students live in a supportive environment and work closely with other students to develop their abilities. On the contrary, they are lonely places where students lose faith in themselves. Too often, students wander anonymously through the corridors and classes without ever receiving a kind word from a teacher who actually understands their circumstances.

The architects of massive high schools, focused as they were on the business commandment to grow as a means of cutting costs and achieving variety, apparently forgot that young people are happiest and perform best in a relatively small world where their teachers know them and their parents and where students know each other. When parents and teachers collaborate to nurture each student, and when students comfortably work together to learn material, students begin to develop a sense of belonging. Sustained by positive relationships with classmates and teachers, they learn to believe in themselves and to value academic achievement.

Realizing the liabilities of vast high schools that discourage learning and breed alienation, the Baltimore school system is dismantling nine high schools consisting of up to 2,000 students each. A five-year, $55 million project will break up these high schools and replace them with schools averaging 400–500 students. The new small schools will be located in renovated existing schools, neighborhood buildings, shopping malls, and office buildings and on college campuses.[19] Baltimore has decided against the business commandment to grow. Instead, it has decided to nurture and educate each student in schools built to human scale.

Perhaps the business groups, educators, and parents who willingly consigned students to enormous, factory-like schools beginning in the

1950s would have resisted the business model's mandate to grow had they been aware of the worldview implicit in the discoveries of modern science. That worldview declares that all living systems, including human beings, require interrelatedness, self-organization, and differentiation in order to live and flourish. Interrelatedness, positive relationships with others that encourage and inspire, is found in small schools. Self-organization, the capacity of a living being to shape itself in response to its surroundings, is nurtured best in small schools. Differentiation, the capacity to create infinite variety and to learn from differences, is realized most easily in small schools where children interact comfortably and often. Adhering to these principles gives educators a definite opportunity to achieve excellence. It should be no surprise, given that the push for relentless growth violates the way natural systems operate, that massive schools undermine high standards and drive young people away.

THE BUSINESS COMMANDMENT TO COMPETE GIVES RISE TO CHARTER SCHOOLS

Accepting without question the basic tenet of business that competition prompts efficiency and effectiveness, a great many business leaders, public officials, educators, and parents think that if schools compete with one another for customers, then they will deliver quality education. Confidence in the power of competition has produced charter schools, voucher programs, and for-profit companies. Do these developments further the educational aims of academic excellence and a common culture, or do they seriously threaten them?

Charter Schools: A Coherent Public System of Education?

Charter schools offer a fledgling space for innovation in education. Therefore, it is conceivable that they could transform public education into a reinvigorated, redesigned, highly innovative educational system. Liberated from rigid hierarchical governance and from restrictions imposed by teachers' unions, charter schools have the flexibility to set their own schedules, design their own curricula, respond to the needs of their local communities, and set aside time for teachers to work one-on-one with each student. Furthermore, charter schools are in a position to use the many excellent teaching strategies devised by teachers in traditional public schools. They are free, for example, to experiment with discovery learning, problem-based learning, service learning, school-based instruction, job shadowing, and internships. They are free to ask students to develop portfolios, address genuine community issues, create and run a business, or give a presentation in a public forum. Although statewide standardized achievement tests have pressured countless public teachers into substituting rote memorization for creative teaching, perhaps charter schools are able to resist this pressure. Especially innovative, it seems, are charter schools that belong to larger networks such as those influenced by Ted Sizer and Howard Gardner.

Unlikely though it may be, perhaps all charter schools might one day be united in a new kind of public system of education. Perhaps charter schools—at the same time that they serve the unique needs of individual students, offer distinctive courses and innovative teaching strategies, and respond to the special circumstances of their communities— might also become a coherent public system of education. Perhaps charter schools have the potential to become a united system of separate schools, each of which subscribes to the same basic educational aims and to similar underlying core principles. Fundamental accord among charter schools would address the risk they present of fragmenting society and catering only to the narrow interests of a few.

The potential problems charter schools raise are discussed below. This discussion is not intended as a rejection of charter schools. On the contrary, it is an invitation to charter schools to evaluate themselves as public entities. It is an invitation to provide frequent, complete, and frank disclosure of their successes and limitations. If the general public is to understand and appreciate charter schools, then it is imperative that these schools provide detailed information about their activities. If educators are to learn of successful teaching innovations from these schools, then charter schools must report their successful and unsuccessful practices. Charter schools that tell their own stories fully and explicitly may suggest how everyone in society can participate in educating young people. Their stories may suggest ways that charter schools might cooperate to generate a coherent, unified public system of education that offers every child hope and opportunity.

Individual charter schools need to be transparent. They need to explain to the public how they allocate funds, the qualifications of their teachers, their prevailing instructional strategies, their methods of assessment, the content of courses, the time teachers spend conferring with individual students, how teachers and administrators relate to one another, actions that join the school with the community, governance practices, problems a school encounters, and notable successes. By fully and frequently describing their work, charter schools become their own vocal advocates.

CHARTER SCHOOLS: WHAT THEY ARE AND WHY THEY HAVE DEVELOPED

Chester E. Finn, one of the founders of Edison Schools, Inc., a private company that manages charter schools, describes charter schools as being free from state and local regulations. Independent and self-governing, they have "control over their own curriculum and instruction." They are fiscally independent. They make all personnel decisions and control "internal organization, calendar, schedule, and much more."[20] Charter schools need *not* be staffed by trained teachers or managed by a school board and superintendent.[21]

Anyone can found such a school. It is important to realize that at present and quite intentionally "the charter school idea . . . rejects the 'one best system.' . . . *Schools should be different in myriad ways,* and all families should be able to choose among them."[22]

In the 1990s, nearly forty states passed laws to permit the creation of charter schools. The charter school movement has grown from two charter schools in Minnesota in 1992 "to more than 2,300 schools in 37 states and the District of Columbia as of the 2000–2001 academic year."[23] A charter school is founded when a group—virtually any group—decides to create a unique school that is designed to attract a certain clientele. A charter, or contract, is drawn up between the founders and the public body that grants the charter. Those founding a charter school typically sign a five-year contract with the state.[24] This contract describes "the conditions under which the school will operate and the goals it must accomplish in order to remain in operation.

Schools that fail to live up to the promises set forth in the charter risk being closed."[25] These schools are springing up all over the country, changing the fundamental nature of public education.

Charter schools compete for customers. The assumption is that competition will cause these schools to provide quality education. However, many authorities, such as historian Carl Kaestle, explain that we have no reason to believe that competition will lead to better schools.[26] Just because, like companies, competitive charter schools win happy customers, it does not necessarily follow that they deliver quality education. What charter schools do deliver are curricula that serve the interests of their respective founders.

Parents are attracted, understandably, by a uniquely designed school that seems to address their children's peculiar needs and interests. They may choose a charter school because it features certain subjects or programs suitable for their children. Or they may enroll their children in a charter school because they have ceased hoping that the traditional public school in their area will improve. Although assuredly traditional public schools can be improved, as I show elsewhere, still it is understandable that parents should view charter schools as an attractive option for their children. Charter schools, however, carry risks. They may shortchange even the satisfied customer and may pose serious difficulties for society. The very autonomy that charter schools insist on is itself problematical.

The intention among members of any group organizing a charter school is that the school shall be autonomous. By definition, any charter school is free, like a business, to define itself and to compete on its own terms. It is free to decide on everything that will attract and keep the customers it seeks. A charter school can decide on such things as its location, furnishings, equipment, textbooks, courses, dress code, class schedule, average class size, activities, and teaching methods. In some states, charter schools are also free to hire nonunion, uncertified teachers. In addition, a charter school is free from the oppressive, top-down, hierarchical bureaucratic structure typical of corporations.

However, in divorcing themselves from the traditional single public school system that extends from state officials through superintendents to principals and teachers, charter schools are also divorcing themselves from the will of the people. The general voice of the people that elects representatives to oversee a single system of education does not affect charter schools.[27] Democracy is irrelevant to their operation. Instead, charter schools exercise local control.

The phrase "local control" applied to charter schools does not necessarily imply community governance. It means that the school's founders, who typically constitute its board of governors, control that school. Charter schools are accountable first to their own board of governors and then to their customers. Only traditional public schools are accountable to the vote of the people. Praising the autonomy of charter schools, their supporters explain that charter schools give ordinary people the opportunity to govern their own educational affairs. People get to focus a charter school on what matters to them.[28] In reality, however, localism cannot always be trusted to safeguard the rights of a charter school's customers or its community. America's history contains little evidence that local institutions are more disposed to protect individual rights than state or federal institutions are.

How Good Are Charter Schools? Can We Tell?

In theory, the boards of charter schools are supposed to report to the public bodies that grant them charters. Although each state is supposed to monitor its charter schools, most states fail to do so.[29] In states that do hold charter schools accountable for achieving mutually agreed-on outcomes, the usual measure of success is that of high marks on standardized achievement tests. Another measure of success for charter schools is that of customer satisfaction. If customer satisfaction is high, then chances are that a charter school will keep its doors open even if test scores are low. It is almost inconceivable that a state would shut down a charter school praised enthusiastically by happy clients.

When test scores and customer satisfaction send different messages, accountability becomes murky. The responses of students in Michigan reveal that most of them believed that attending charter schools had improved their academic performance. Unfortunately, they were mistaken. Their scores on standardized achievement tests had not shown gains in their academic performance.[30] It is significant that disappointing test scores did not reduce the satisfaction students expressed. Apparently, customer satisfaction is not convincing evidence that a school actually furthers the academic improvement of its students. Happy customers may flock to a successful charter school that fails to help students attain academic excellence. A study of Michigan's charter schools indicates that charter schools generally produce inferior academic outcomes compared with traditional schools—and at greater cost.[31] Just as competition fails to yield academic success, so it fails to yield efficiency and economy. Charter schools in Michigan "receive more money than traditional public schools offering similar services and serving similar populations."[32]

Michigan is not the only state offering warning signals that dampen enthusiasm for charter schools. The Brookings Institute has gathered data on the performance of charter schools across the nation. A review of reading and math achievement test scores of 376 charter schools in ten states was conducted by the Brookings Institute in 1999–2000. The data indicate that the math and reading scores of students attending charter schools are significantly lower than the scores of students attending traditional public schools. Fully 59 percent of the students enrolled in traditional public schools scored better than did those attending charter schools.[33] If we are willing to rely on standardized achievement test scores to measure a school's success, then we must conclude that many charter schools are not improving student performance.

Charter Schools Change Society

Charter schools are changing the fundamental structure of American education. They are replacing the traditional single system of public education with a system composed of myriad individual schools, each operating to fulfill its own distinctive purposes. For all Americans, whether they have children in school or not, this change from a single public educational system united in purpose to a collection of autonomous schools following separate paths is of great significance. Abandoning a single system of public education designed to accommodate every child may entail abandoning the fundamental principles on which that one system is based. It may mean abandoning the idea that public schools exist both to serve the well-being of every child and to forge a common culture.

America's public schools have long taught young people, however imperfectly, that their personal, private welfare is not the only thing that matters. The good of the whole community, of every member, is equally important.[34] To reject traditional public schools, with their attempt to convey a shared vision of civic responsibility, is to gamble that from an array of schools sharing neither principle nor curriculum can emerge a coherent, unified culture that embraces every citizen. Jonathan Kozol cautions, "Think of cities that are just struggling to hold together . . . and then imagine what it would be like if you added a system whereby every little intellectual, ethnic, theological splinter group could indoctrinate children separately, and use public money to do it. It would rip apart the social fabric of this nation."[35] Unlike traditional schools that educate an extraordinarily diverse society, charter schools are able to target the exclusive interests of a few. In doing so, they have the power, should they wish to exercise it, to sort and exclude students.[36]

Unfortunately, many charter schools do engage in social sorting, as Gary Miron and Christopher Nelson, research associates at Western Michigan University's Evaluation Center, point out. Miron and Nelson have evaluated charter schools in Michigan, Pennsylvania, Connecticut, and Illinois. Their research shows that disparities exist in the types of students attending charter and noncharter schools. They note that Michigan charter schools often limit access on the basis of race, ethnicity, income, and ability. Limiting student access, sorting and segregating young people, occurs in part because when charter schools locate in affluent areas, as more and more of them are doing, they automatically exclude poor minorities.[37] Segregation also occurs in part because, like private schools, charter schools are free to develop their own standards and expectations and to advise applicants to look elsewhere when they do not meet these standards. Like private schools, charter schools choose their students. They cannot refuse admission, as do private schools, but they can counsel young people to look elsewhere. The phrases "We cannot provide your child with the services she deserves" and "Our difficult courses might put your child at an unfortunate disadvantage" exemplify discouraging words that courteously reject applicants. Although all charter schools taken together may cover a "full, heterogeneous range of educational concerns," their range of specialties means nothing to the child a school prefers not to serve.[38] Choice is not merely the customer's. It is exercised by schools as well as their clients. Only traditional public schools accept everyone.

Although charter schools are not without problems, some of them certainly offer students a fine education. The highly regarded Coalition for Essential Schools, for example, is justly praised for inspiring young people to develop their intellectual abilities and unique talents. Perhaps individual charter schools might one day metamorphose into a new form of unified public school system that gives every student in every charter school an equitable opportunity to discover what they can become. If charter schools are transparent and accountable, then their innovations may initiate a new version of a single, common system of public education for the twenty-first century.

THE BUSINESS COMMANDMENT TO SET TARGETS AND STRESS ACCOUNTABILITY HAS PRODUCED STANDARDIZED ACHIEVEMENT TESTS: SHOULD PARENTS BE GLAD?

Business is gaining control of education in America. We have seen that the business commandment to compete has produced selective charter schools, and the business commandment to grow has produced immense, impersonal schools that drive students away. The business commandment to reach measurable targets has also had unfortunate consequences. It has resulted in statewide standardized achievement tests that give us a distorted picture of student performance. Scores on these tests have recently become—in virtually every publicly funded elementary school in America, whether a traditional school or a charter school—the sole measure of academic success. Schools that earn high scores are rewarded, and those that receive low scores are penalized. Because success is defined by test scores, it is everyone's responsibility to make certain that these tests measure exactly what students are supposed to know. It is everyone's responsibility to make sure that preparing for these tests actually improves the educational experience schools offer children.

Business Targets and Tests

In these early years of the twenty-first century, running a business is synonymous with achieving measurable targets. Business leaders use quantification to establish objectives and to control the organization's progress toward these targets. They consider that "to run an organiza-tion, a living system, entails . . . a quantitative summing up of the sep-arate contributions of each part" as these parts contribute, or fail to con-tribute, to the company's ultimate target.[39] Such thinking ignores, of course, the interrelatedness, the systemic nature, of the parts of an or-ganization. It ignores the fact that human beings weave patterns as they relate to one another and that from these patterns there emerges a whole far greater than, and distinct from, the sum of its parts.[40]

Whenever our quantitative interventions in any organization disrupt the patterns that relationships naturally form, the system is impaired. Furthermore, when a business, or a division within a business, suc-cessfully meets externally imposed targets, that success reveals nothing about the inner workings of the organization. A company that meets its measurable targets may be infected with gross inefficiency, waste, in-ferior quality, and employee discontent. Those who focus on quantifi-able targets, and who use these targets to punish and reward people within the organization, are overlooking the essential point. The health and strength of relationships within the organization are responsible for its long-term success. Nurture the relationships, and the end will take care of itself.[41]

Standardized achievement tests are education's equivalent of the measurable targets that are common to business. The 2 January 2002 No Child Left Behind Act establishes scoring high on standardized achievement tests as the definitive target for all children to reach in grades three–eight.[42] Evidently, policy makers and business alliances, removed though they are from actual classrooms, are convinced that a score on a single standardized achievement test is sufficient to reveal the extent of a child's understanding of academic material. They are convinced that from test scores they can draw sound inferences about the competence of a school's teachers and its principal.

These standardized achievement test scores are widely used to assess the academic improvement of children in charter schools. If students in charter schools indicate customer satisfaction but do not score well on achievement tests, then the conclusion is that the schools are deficient. Could it be that the school offers experiences that cannot be measured? Test scores, an abstraction, reveal nothing about what principals and teachers actually do in their schools or about what children feel and accomplish. The daily life of any school and the relationships of all its members decide whether or not its children develop and flourish.

Recognizing the need to use many approaches to assess student achievement, educators worked indefatigably in the mid 1980s and throughout the 1990s to develop challenging teaching and assessment strategies: "Classroom approaches such as portfolios, project-based teaching, and performance-based testing . . . blossomed."[43] These approaches succeeded because they encourage all children to develop their talents and because they give all children many pathways to achieve and demonstrate academic proficiency.[44] These assessment strategies were used in conjunction with standardized achievement tests in many states. Nevertheless, today "state governors and legislatures have moved swiftly to . . . measure performance [exclusively] through standardized tests" and to hold teachers and administrators accountable for student outcomes on these tests.[45]

Just as a business that concentrates on reaching measurable targets by any means does so at the expense of quality products and a harmonious culture, so a school district that concentrates on measurable targets does so at the expense of high academic standards and a rich educational experience for young people. As a subject-area specialist for a county in Florida has written, "FCAT, the Florida high-stakes test, drives everything in education in this state. Schools do very little creative teaching."[46] Several questions are posed by high-stakes tests. Do scores accurately show what children have learned? Do the tests cause students to learn less than they deserve to know? Do children learn to reason, figure things out, examine problems, answer questions, and appreciate art and music because of high-stakes tests? Do high-stakes tests justify drawing inferences about an instructor's teaching ability? How trustworthy are the tests, anyway?

The Disturbing Truth about Standardized Achievement Tests

Five national standardized achievement tests are now used widely in public schools: California Achievement Tests, Comprehensive Tests of Basic Skills, Iowa Tests of Basic Skills, Metropolitan Achievement Tests, and Stanford Achievement Tests. Although the names of some of these tests imply that they are designed by university faculty or government experts, in reality they are produced and marketed by private companies. For example, the Iowa Tests of Basic Skills is made by the Riverside Publishing Company, and McGraw-Hill produces the Comprehensive Tests of Basic Skills.[47]

Each of these private companies produces "off-the-shelf," one-size-fits-all, standardized achievement tests. These generic tests are currently being used in many states in spite of the stipulation in the 2002 Education Act that states must adjust commercial tests to reflect their own state content standards. Tight budgets compel a number of states to forgo customized tests.[48]

Mass-produced, generic tests cannot possibly ask germane questions, of course, that bear on the specific content that teachers in each state have agreed to teach.[49] If a test is generic, its questions may not cover, say, the particular math problems students have learned. A fifth grade math teacher may teach brilliantly the specific content required in her state, only to find that standardized achievement tests omit a good deal of the material her state wanted fifth graders to master. Her students then get low scores, not because they were poorly taught and not because they did not learn but simply because they were tested on irrelevant material. Even customized tests contain questions that fail to cover the content children have been asked to learn.[50] Those who stand behind high-stakes testing need to look closely at the tests they are making students take.

The Norm-Referenced Test: Designed to Limit Student Success

Many schools use *norm-referenced* standardized achievement tests. This "off-the-shelf" variety of standardized test is relatively cheap and easy to administer. The norm-referenced test is *not* designed to show how well students have learned an academic subject: "The objective is to spread out the scores as much as possible . . . [to] ensure that *not* everyone will be able to answer a given question. . . . [Norm-referenced tests include] questions that are answered correctly by only some students."[51] Norm-referenced tests are *not* meant to be a real measure of the achievements of students or the talents of teachers.[52] On the contrary, norm-referenced tests are designed to compare test takers to one another.

If all members of a sixth grade class taking a test were to answer the same four reading questions correctly, then their parents might conclude that the sixth grade teacher had done a fine job of helping these children acquire the reading skills that their state and school district expected them to acquire. Test makers, however, would conclude that those four questions had to be eliminated from the next edition of the text precisely because all of the sixth graders did get them right. The test makers always remove answers that most students get right: "The more important the content, the more likely teachers are to stress it. The more teachers stress important content, the better students will do on an item measuring that content. But the better students do on such an item, the more likely it is that the item will disappear from the test."[53] For example, test makers will eliminate from next year's fourth grade test the vocabulary words that students know well, and in their place they will include words that are not taught, words that only 40–60 percent of the students can answer correctly. Because items on a norm-referenced test are meticulously designed so that only 40–60 percent of the students are likely to answer them correctly, that test is sabotaging teacher and student alike.

Criterion-Referenced Tests

An alternative to the generic, norm-referenced tests is the criterion-referenced test, also known as "standards based" because it is based on content standards developed in each state. It compares each student to a set standard. Unlike norm-referenced tests, which compare students to each other, criterion-referenced tests do ask some questions that deal with a state's specific curricular goals, known as "content standards."[54] Customized, criterion-referenced tests actually attempt to discover something definite about student proficiency. Although these tests lack some of the blatant deficiencies of norm-referenced tests, nevertheless, they share with them a number of problems. A review of these problems makes it clear that parents and politicians have a responsibility to our children to ask: "Should standardized achievement test scores be the target that decides the success of students, teachers, principals, and superintendents?" The answer is a resounding *no*.

Standardized Achievement Questions Ignore Course Content

One problem with all standardized achievement tests is that they seem invariably to contain a number of items that have nothing to do with course material. These items are the kinds of questions contained on intelligence tests. They exist to assess aptitude, not knowledge. An aptitude item is one that the test taker can figure out by applying his or her existing knowledge. No prior study is necessary. For example, an aptitude item might ask sixth grade students: "If someone really wants to conserve resources, one good way to do so is to (A) Leave lights on even if they are not needed; (B) Wash small loads instead of large loads in a clothes washing machine; (C) Write on both sides of the paper; (D) Place used newspapers in the garbage." The answer is C because it describes an act of conservation. If a person knows the meaning of *conserve,* that person can answer the question correctly. Success has nothing to do with course content and everything to do with verbal facility.[55]

Who is most likely to respond correctly to questions that stress verbal facility? Who will find it relatively easy to use vocabulary words that come not from the classroom but, rather, from everyday life? Questions that call on outside knowledge favor those from affluent backgrounds. The children of low-income parents living in Appalachia or inner-city Detroit are not likely to speak and write Standard English with ease, any more than the children of recent immigrants from Vietnam, Mexico, or Russia are. If, however, a child's parent is a middle-class citizen of the suburbs, then that child has probably grown up hearing a varied use of Standard English. Such a child will easily recognize words and sentences that are difficult for children from low-income families. Questions based on outside knowledge are therefore discriminatory. They do not measure simply what children learn in school. They reflect who the child is—the child's race, ethnicity, and social level.

Standardized achievement tests misrepresent student mastery of material, then, because they do not examine students exclusively on the content they have studied. As we have seen, they include items that come from outside the curriculum, items that favor students from prosperous families. They also contain many questions that evaluate aptitude, not command of content. The brevity of standardized achievement tests is also problematical. Because children cannot sit still for more than an hour, their standardized test must be brief. Therefore, this brief test will necessarily exclude a great deal of material. Very likely it will eliminate some material that the children have studied, and instead it will include content that their teacher deemed relatively unimportant in relation to all the topics to be covered.[56] It is impossible in a short test to give students a fair chance to reveal the true extent of their knowledge and understanding.

How Tests Affect Children

According to W. James Popham, who for years headed a group that created high-stakes tests for more than a dozen states, no sound standardized achievement test exists.[57] Because existing tests are flawed, it is impossible to infer from test scores the depth of a child's understanding or the extent of a child's knowledge. Test scores should not be the sole basis for judging a student's achievement or a school's quality. And yet, as we have seen in the discussion of charter schools, they are used as the primary criterion for evaluating the effectiveness of these schools. They are also used in most states to determine the success or failure of traditional public schools. In Florida, "schools whose students scored high on a state-developed achievement test . . . [are] assigned grades of A. Schools whose students scored badly . . . [get] grades of F."[58] The F-graded school in Florida, as in many states, is penalized, and the school whose students perform well is rewarded.

The arbitrary threat of rewards and punishments restrains principals from practicing creative leadership, demeans teachers, and short-changes students. The pressure on young people to earn high test scores for the good of the school gives them a distorted impression of what education is about and a limited idea of their own abilities. Children who earn low test scores are defeated by these tests. They regard a low score as incontrovertible evidence that they are less intelligent than their classmates. They see themselves as stupid and unworthy. They believe that they are fated to get bad grades.

These discouraged children, trapped in a world that exists to attain target test scores, do not have a chance to discover that intelligence is not fixed but, rather, grows as a result of experience. Subjected to repetitive drills and other practices devoted to succeeding on standardized tests, children are denied learning opportunities that help them find out that determination, perseverance, curiosity, imagination, insight, and the opportunity to learn in their own way at their own pace will enable them to excel in school and in life.

Children who easily earn high marks are also harmed. They become falsely confident of their intellectual prowess. Methods of preparing for achievement tests have deprived them of rich educational experiences. Consequently, these children have not been challenged. They have not had opportunities to discover their own strengths and limitations. Their full potential remains untapped. If society wants students to learn, and to enjoy learning, and if society wants them to become reflective, knowledgeable, compassionate people, then society must support a stimulating learning environment. Such an environment invites students to be active, responsible learners, not passive test takers within the classroom, not merely on preparing to earn high test scores.

Testing That Benefits Children

Schools around the country have proved that when teachers work together to develop varied methods of assessment, and when these assessment methods carry as much weight as scores on standardized tests, students discover the joy of learning for its own sake. They enjoy school and do well because the importance of other kinds of tests tempers the oppressive demand that they excel on a statewide test. A true learning community where students flourish "not only preserves and nourishes the individuals who compose it, but also underscores the relationships among these individuals. . . . Children develop a genuine commitment to each other and to the 'us' composed of these real people."[59]

Politicians, business groups, and some educators wave aside evidence that teaching only to the target of high test scores is a mistake. They dismiss growing concern among most educators that quality education and student well-being are actually eroded by aiming at the target of reaching high scores on standardized achievement tests. They resist the claim that setting up the target of high scores on standardized achievement tests is an inadequate basis for deciding a school's future. Are they depriving children of a real education for the quick fix of attaining a measurable target?

Parents Know Better

In theory, according to the business model that equates success with reaching measurable targets, using the target of scores on achievement tests to measure quality education makes sense. To a great many parents, however, using test scores to measure quality education is a harmful practice. Parents and educators across the nation are increasingly troubled by the demand of the 2002 education bill that a quality education be equated with a high score on a standardized test: "There is a growing national backlash over what many parents and teachers consider excessive focus on standardized tests."[60] Parents notice that because standardized tests cover only mathematics, reading, and writing (and, in a few states, science), these are the subjects that receive special emphasis. Music, art, physical education, and social studies receive relatively limited attention, if any. But what if a child loves those subjects? When the target of earning high test scores dictates the courses to be taught, schools stop teaching to the range of student interests and abilities. They stop inventing imaginative lessons that speak to the multiple ways in which students are intelligent. In the past, individual teachers had the latitude to nurture every student. Today their work is driven not by their students' needs and abilities but, rather, by their own need to make sure that their students get the right answers on multiple-choice tests.

Parents are discovering that the kind of teaching that produces high test scores makes their children resent school. Repetitious instruction and boring drills smother student interest. Repeated practice taking multiple-choice tests dulls curiosity and imagination. This time would be better spent, according to parents, on projects and apprenticeships that inspire a clear understanding of reading, writing, and mathematics.

In declaring standardized achievement test scores to be the ultimate target to be reached by schools, policy makers are equating education with regurgitating facts on tests. However, many parents are unconvinced that a child's high test score really signifies that a school has given that child a quality education. Parents know that their children's educational experience cannot be fathomed by test scores. Are children learning critical thinking, curiosity, and problem-solving techniques? Are they learning compassion, patience, and the ability to get along with others? Are they developing confidence in their own abilities and trust that they can excel? None of these things can be measured, but they are too important to be neglected as young people acquire such essential skills as reading and writing. Mindful of what standardized achievement tests fail to measure, parents in affluent Marin County, California, gave their children, who had in the past scored well on standardized tests, waivers exempting them from further testing. Their contention is that these tests undermine quality education.[61]

Measurable Targets Sabotage Quality Education

I have shown that it is impossible to infer from test scores how much children have learned and that it is impossible to infer from test scores how well schools are teaching children. Assigning great importance to the scores students earn on standardized achievement tests has diminished, not improved, the quality of American education. Those who insist on giving these tests should consider Alfie Kohn's conclusions: "Tests should not be timed. They should not be given to young children. They should not be given too frequently. They should not be norm-referenced or reported in such a way as to emphasize rankings rather than absolute scores. They should not consist of multiple-choice questions. They should be designed to tap students' understanding of ideas rather than their ability to memorize lists of facts and definitions."[62]

Unfortunately, the standardized achievement tests in vogue today violate these precepts. Their damage is obvious. A seven-year-old from Illinois whom I met on a plane said that he hoped he could live forever with the grandmother he was traveling to visit for the summer. Asked why, he said, "School is just work, work, work. It's not the teacher's fault. It's the test. Maybe where grandma lives, school is better." He was looking, of course, for joy in learning. Classrooms ruled solely, or even primarily, by the target of earning high scores on standardized achievement tests do not invite young people to talk excitedly about their learning adventures or even to have exciting learning adventures. Like businesses, schools have become workplaces driven by an externally imposed target; and, as in businesses, those being forced to attain these measurable targets live in a world of joyless stress and pressure where original thinking is subordinated to doing what has been decreed from above.

BUSINESSES RUN SCHOOLS: EDUCATIONAL MANAGEMENT ORGANIZATIONS

Business is *indirectly* gaining control of public education as the business model of growing, competing, and reaching targets is imposed on K–12 schools. Business is also gaining *direct* control of public education in the form of educational management organizations, called EMOs. School boards and the founders of publicly supported charters are outsourcing education to EMOs in the same way that Ford outsources the manufacture of bumpers to such companies as Visteon. In turning public schools over to private companies, they are making accountability the private activity of the for-profit institution rather than a matter for the community to govern. This is questionable policy, given that EMOs exist expressly to profit from educating young people. Can the general public be confident that when a business runs a school, it will put quality education ahead of its own profit?

Research is beginning to suggest that when for-profit companies run public schools, whether tax-supported charters or traditional public schools, the companies' own financial gains will always take precedence over improving education. EMOs, for the sake of the bottom line, will shortchange students. For example, when Edison Schools, Inc., came to San Francisco in 1998, the San Francisco Board of Education asked it to take over management of a troubled traditional public elementary school. In 2001 the Board of Education revoked Edison's contract, which ran through 2003, on the grounds that Edison had forced out poorly performing students by encouraging them to attend other schools. Systematically, this for-profit company urged the parents of weak students to send their children elsewhere.[63] The San Francisco school board realized that the EMO was rejecting disadvantaged students and that for this reason, and not because of superior instruction, the school's test scores had improved.

Like Edison, Educational Alternatives Inc. (EAI) has also put profit ahead of quality education. From 1992 to 1995, EAI ran nine traditional public schools for the city of Baltimore, Maryland. Baltimore paid EAI $5,400 per pupil, and in return EAI agreed to boost test scores.[64] A publicly held company with obligations to shareholders, EAI cut costs by hiring inexperienced interns, by severely curtailing services available to the learning disabled, and by eliminating music and art programs. EAI's cost-cutting measures, which drove its stock price up from $4.00 to $49.00 per share, reduced important services, diluted the curriculum, and, not surprisingly, failed to improve student performance. The performance of EAI students on standardized achievement tests was no better than that of their peers attending district-run Baltimore public schools. Therefore, in 1995 Baltimore cancelled its contract with EAI.[65] Undaunted, EAI signed a contract in 1997 with the state of Arizona to run at least a dozen schools.

Whether EMOs govern traditional public schools or publicly funded charter schools, they have difficulty improving student performance. In Michigan, for example, the test score gains in EMO charter schools have been below those in non-EMO schools.[66] This disappointing result causes some concern over the news that 75 percent of the charters approved by Florida in one year went to EMOs. "Buyer beware" seems an appropriate warning not only for those contemplating hiring EMOs but also for those eager to apply a business model to education.

BUSINESS AND EDUCATION FOR ALL

Confidence in market forces and distrust of public responsibility for education have combined to threaten America's educational system. Taxpayer dollars that were originally designated to finance traditional public schools are being diverted to finance charter schools and voucher programs and also to pay educational management organizations to educate the nation's young people. The use of taxpayer money for these purposes suggests that the word *public* is acquiring a new meaning in the twenty-first century.

Chester F. Finn says that charter schools are public, even though they are not part of what he calls a "moribund, government-run, bureaucratic system of public education."[67] They are public, even though they are not run by democratically elected officials representing the will of the people. Finn calls charter schools public because they are "open to the public and paid for by the public."[68] Perhaps in this sense they are public. And yet charter schools are not public, really, because they exist exclusively to serve the private interests of the local groups that design them and are thus positioned to be indifferent to the public good.

The term *public education,* once reserved for traditional public schools, is also applied today to charter schools overseen by educators and community members, and charter schools that have been outsourced by state officials to private EMOs. These outsourced schools are called "public" presumably because tax dollars are used to pay EMOs for managing them. They are not public, however, in the sense of being accountable to the public, for an EMO, a private company, has more or less complete control of the educational process that goes on inside the school building.

"Public education" originally signified "common schools." They were called "common" schools because they served the entire population, and they were common because they tried, however falteringly, to forge a common culture. Public schools were termed "common," too, because they strove to inculcate in young people the notion that as members of a unified culture—namely, a democratic society—citizens were responsible not only for their own well-being but also for the well-being of others.

Today we are in danger of losing the notion of public education as education that forges a common culture. We have progressed far on the road to abandoning America's traditional single system of public—common—education. In its place we are developing a new concept of public education as a collection of separate schools, each pursuing its own private interests and many of which are run by for-profit EMOs intent on profit and indifferent to the needs of children.

Adherence to a business model has contributed to this narrow concept of public education. A business model urges schools to grow, compete, set measurable targets, and dispense rewards and punishments. A business model also seeks private benefits and profit. As we have seen, business practices cannot be counted on to generate academic excellence, draw forth the full potential of every student, or communicate to a diverse people a shared vision of a common culture. Business does not inculcate in young people a sense of responsibility for America's democratic society. Business does not improve academic performance and unify a diverse people in schools that are run democratically, by the people.

The business model that requires growth, competition, targets, and accountability does not assure quality education. Private businesses (EMOs) that have taken over the management of public schools cannot be depended upon to deliver quality education. A model derived from modern science, however, might help us transform traditional public schools into learning environments where each child thrives.

NOTES

1. Larry Cuban, "Introduction" to "A Nation at Risk?" in Sheila Curran Bernard and Sarah Mondale, *School: The Story of American Public Education,* ed. Sarah Mondale and Sarah B. Patton (Boston: Beacon Press, 2001), 174.

2. Cuban, "Introduction," 176.

3. Cuban, "Introduction," 179.

4. Donella Meadows, "Economics Laws Clash with the Planet's," *Timeline,* no. 57 (May-June 2001): 8–9.

5. H. Thomas Johnson and Anders Broms, *Profit beyond Measure: Extraordinary Results through Attention to Work and People* (New York: Free Press, 2000), 34–42.

6. See Keith H. Hammonds, "Size Is Not a Strategy," *Fast Company,* September 2002: 78–86.

7. John E. Chubb and Terry M. Moe, *Politics, Markets, and America's Schools* (Washington, D.C.: Brookings Institution, 1990), 34.

8. Louis Menand, *The Metaphysical Club: A Story of Ideas in America* (New York: Farrar, Straus and Giroux, 2001), 301, 303. The universal principles of interrelatedness and self-organization confirm that natural behavior involves collaboration, not competition.

9. Lester Ward, *Dynamic Sociology,* cited in Menand, *The Metaphysical Club,* 303.

10. W. Edwards Deming, *The New Economics* (Cambridge: MIT Center for Advance Engineering Study, 1994), 121.

11. Deming, *The New Economics,* 73.

12. Richard Ely, "The Past and Present of Political Economy," cited in Menand, *The Metaphysical Club,* 303.

13. W. Edwards Deming, cited in Peter Senge, "View from the Chair," *Reflections* 4 (winter 2002): 79.

14. Chubb and Moe, *Politics, Markets, and America's Schools,* 104.

15. Patricia A. Wasley, "Small Classes, Small Schools: The Time Is Now," *Educational Leadership* 59, no. 5 (February 2002): 8.

16. Diane Ravitch, *Left Back: A Century of Battles over School Reform* (New York: Simon and Schuster, 2000), 458; Lawrence A. Cremin, *American Education: The Metropolitan Experience, 1876–1980* (New York: Harper and Row, 1988), 647–50.

17. Bruce J. Biddle and David C. Berliner, "Small Class Size and Its Effects," *Educational Leadership* 59, no. 5 (February 2002): 23; Tom Vander Ark, "The Case for Small High Schools," *Educational Leadership* 59, no. 5 (February 2002): 55–59; Rick Allen, "Big Schools: The Way We Are," *Educational Leadership* 59, no. 5 (February 2002): 36–41.

18. Ravitch, *Left Back*, 458.

19. Gary Gately, "Maryland: A Move for Smaller Schools," *The New York Times*, 10 October 2001, available at www.ruraledu.org/keep-learning.cfm? record-no+6141.

20. Chester E. Finn Jr., Bruno V. Manno, and Gregg Vanourek, *Charter Schools in Action: Renewing Public Education* (Princeton: Princeton University Press, 2000), 15–16.

21. Finn, Manno, and Vanourek, *Charter Schools in Action*, 16.

22. Finn, Manno, and Vanourek, *Charter Schools in Action*, 61.

23. Gary Miron and Christopher Nelson, *What's Public about Charter Schools? Lessons Learned about Choice and Accountability* (Thousand Oaks, Calif.: Corwin Press, Inc., 2002), 2.

24. Sheila Curran Bernard and Sarah Mondale, *School: The Story of American Education*, ed. Sarah Mondale and Sarah B. Patton (Boston: Beacon Press, 2001), 205.

25. Miron and Nelson, *What's Public about Charter Schools?* 3.

26. Carl Kaestle, cited in Bernard and Mondale, *School*, 205.

27. The crippling bureaucracy inherited from business that hampers traditional public schools can be eliminated without replacing America's traditional single system of public education. A traditional single system of education can reduce directives from school boards and superintendents and suspend regulations while still sharing fundamental educational aims with other public schools and school districts. New York's East Harlem school district, for example, gave the district's best teachers space in existing school buildings to house the schools that they were invited to design according to their professional judgment. Their new schools replaced the district's failing schools. Experienced professional teachers made educational decisions about specific goals within the context of the traditional public school system. If managers of school districts resisted the temptation to emulate business by issuing top-down directives, and if instead they freed people to do the work they were trained to do, then bureaucracy would not be a problem. See Bernard and Mondale, *School*, 180.

28. Chubb and Moe, *Politics, Markets, and America's Schools*, 3–4.

29. Bernard and Mondale, *School*, 205.

30. Miron and Nelson, *What's Public about Charter Schools?* 200

31. Miron and Nelson, *What's Public about Charter Schools?* 205.

32. Miron and Nelson, *What's Public about Charter Schools?* 204.

33. *NCCSR Bookmark* 3, no. 9 (September 2002), available at www.goodschools.gwu.edu/pubs/book/sep02.html (accessed 10 March 2002).

34. Miron and Nelson, *What's Public about Charter Schools?* 11.

35. Jonathan Kozol, cited in Bernard and Mondale, *School*, 196.

36. Miron and Nelson, *What's Public about Charter Schools?* 6, 12.

37. Miron and Nelson, *What's Public about Charter Schools?* 200.

38. Chubb and Moe, *Politics, Markets, and America's Schools*, 55, 206.

39. Johnson and Broms, *Profit beyond Measure*, 48.

40. Johnson and Broms, *Profit beyond Measure*, 49.

41. Johnson and Broms, *Profit beyond Measure*, 51–58.

42. Alexandra Starr, "Why Johnny Can't Fail," *Business Week*, 25 November 2002: 72–74.

43. Bernard and Mondale, *School*, 180.

44. Elaine B. Johnson, *Contextual Teaching and Learning: What It Is and Why It's Here to Stay* (Thousand Oaks, Calif.: Corwin Press, Inc., 2001), 1–30.

45. Bernard and Mondale, *School*, 178–79.

46. Laura Snow, "State Tests" (2 January 1998), personal e-mail, 2 January 2003.

47. W. James Popham, *The Truth about Testing: An Educator's Call to Action* (Alexandria: Association for Supervision and Curriculum Development, 2001), 49, 74.

48. Starr, "Why Johnny Can't Fail," 74.

49. Ravitch, *Left Back*, 123, 131, 160.

50. Popham, *The Truth about Testing*, 39.

51. Alfie Kohn, *The Case against Standardized Testing: Raising the Scores, Ruining the Schools* (Portsmouth, N.Y.: Heinemann, 2000), 36, emphasis added.

52. Popham, *The Truth about Testing*, 11.

53. Popham, *The Truth about Testing*, 48.

54. Kohn, *The Case against Standardized Testing*, 14.

55. Popham, *The Truth about Testing*, 71.

56. Popham, *The Truth about Testing*, 34, 56, 60, 65, 71.

57. Popham, *The Truth about Testing*, 32–34.

58. Popham, *The Truth about Testing,* 34.

59. Alfie Kohn, *Beyond Discipline: From Compliance to Community* (Alexandria: Association for Supervision and Curriculum Development, 1996), 108.

60. Richard Rothstein, "A School District Refuses to Worship Scores Alone," *The New York Times,* 14 February 2002: A23.

61. Richard Rothstein, "The Growing Revolt against the Tester," *The New York Times,* 30 May 2001: A2.

62. Kohn, *The Case against Standardized Testing,* 45.

63. Edward Wyatt, "Higher Scores Aren't Cure-All, School Run for Profit Learns," *The New York Times,* 13 March 2001: A1–A2.

64. Bernard and Mondale, *School,* 210.

65. Bernard and Mondale, *School,* 203.

66. Miron and Nelson, *What's Public about Charter Schools?* 204.

67. Finn, Manno, and Vanourek, *Charter Schools in Action,* 20, 22.

68. Finn, Manno, and Vanourek, *Charter Schools in Action,* 16.

CHAPTER 3

Modern Science—A Guide to Better Schools

Where shall we turn for guidance as we debate the future of public education in the United States? Although many see in business a sound model for America's educational system, the previous chapters show that applying business practices to education generates serious problems. Modern science, however, has made discoveries that do apply to education. Working from many different angles in biology, chemistry, and physics—especially the branch of physics known as evolutionary cosmology—scientists have arrived at remarkable new insights that affect how we think about daily life. Among the most striking of these insights is the suggestion that certain universal principles are at work on Earth and throughout the cosmos.[1] These principles offer a refreshing new perspective from which to view public education in the twenty-first century. Applying them to education has the potential to transform traditional public schools into rich learning environments that give every child an equal opportunity to excel.

Most of us go through each day without noticing the elaborate worldview—the web of ideas—that prompts us to support a politician, agree with a friend, or see meaning in an action. Nevertheless, our personal worldview is such an essential part of who we are that many of us shut our minds against new information that challenges it. We reject new possibilities. This chapter invites readers to think about the new possibilities for education present in the three universal principles emerging from modern science. It challenges public officials, parents, and educators to embrace a new way of thinking that has the potential to revive public education.[2]

THE NEWTONIAN WORLDVIEW

Perhaps long immersion in the Newtonian worldview causes many to resist new insights derived from modern science. After all, the Newtonian view of the universe has for over three centuries dominated Western thinking about government, business, and educational organizations. Indebted to Copernicus, Galileo Galilei, Rene Descartes, and Isaac Newton, the Newtonian view of reality holds that the universe is dualistic. That is, spirit and matter are separate; mind and body are separate. Spirit is intrinsically valuable, but matter, devoid of spiritual significance, is not. According to the Newtonian scheme of things, the universe is an impersonal machine in which all matter operates according to mechanical laws. These inexorable mechanical laws care nothing for human beings.

Irrelevant to the workings of this great machine, like insignificant bits of dust, human beings are separate from the dynamics of the planet they inhabit and observe. From a Newtonian perspective, the human mind, the "I" that observes the physical world, exists apart from that world. Because the external world does exist apart from human consciousness, human beings are capable of objectively observing and recording it. The world is "out there," and thus the "task of the scientist is to observe the 'out there' as objectively as possible."[3]

The external world of objects that scientists observe is solid, according to Newton, because it consists of atoms, and atoms are made up of solid particles. "If we could break into the atom," Newtonian physicists speculated at the close of the nineteenth century, "then it is entirely probable that we would find inside of it the basic building block out of which all things are made." The idea of a basic building block is clear if we imagine a unique red brick out of which everything is made— from stars, trees, water, and freeways to chipmunks and ice cream cones. For decades scientists worked to get inside the atom, expecting to find inert matter there. When they did penetrate the atom, however, they were astonished and perplexed to find not matter but, in fact, mainly empty space containing minuscule particles that vibrate and move, as if they were flashing in and out of existence.[4] This discovery forced scientists to reject the Newtonian explanation of the universe. Newton's laws still seemed to apply to big stuff, but they simply did not apply to subatomic phenomena. They did not, therefore, explain the nature of reality.

WHAT IS REALITY? THE QUANTUM VIEW

The subject of quantum physics tends to be shrouded in mystery and misconception. This is in part because of the advanced mathematics that details the full theory and in part because quantum physics describes a reality that defies common sense. The basic view of reality required to make sense of experiments in quantum physics significantly challenges conventional thinking. It challenges dramatically the way we look at the world and the way we understand our relationship to the world. Our fundamental notions of the identity, locality, and even the reality of objects no longer hold in the usual way.[5]

Quantum physics shows, for example, that the relationships among particles in an atom do not conform to the principles of classical Newtonian physics. Classical physics says that it is possible to measure both the position and the momentum of an object as it moves in space and, thus, to predict where the object will be at some point in the future. If we know an airplane's position and its momentum, for example, then we can predict when it will reach its destination. However, we cannot know at the same time both the position and the momentum of a subatomic particle. A subatomic particle is a "quantum"—a quantity of something that we cannot analyze as if it were a solid object visible to the naked eye.[6] Scientists must choose to measure either a subatomic particle's position or else its momentum. They cannot simultaneously measure both. When scientists are not measuring an electron's position, they cannot say that the electron is in a definite place or traveling on a definite path. They can state its location only as a tendency, a probability. When they do measure an electron's position, it is as though the electron collapses into a small point and occupies a definite place. It may be that the electron reveals itself only if an observer is present. In that sense, relationships create the reality that is observed.

Another way to illustrate this idea was developed by John Wheeler, a Princeton physicist.[7] Wheeler has likened quantum physics to the familiar "Twenty Questions" game. In the *usual* version of the game, one person thinks of an object and holds that object in mind. Others try to guess what the person is thinking about by asking a series of questions that can be answered with *yes* or *no*. For example, if the person is thinking of a coffee cup and is asked, "Is it alive," he or she answers, "No." The game continues until the players have either guessed the object or used up their twenty questions. The key feature of this classical version of the game is that reality is well defined. The idea of "coffee cup" has a definite, independent reality in the person's mind. It exists as a separate, definite entity with its own reality apart from the questioning process.

This version of "Twenty Questions" matches the Newtonian worldview. Things have properties that exist in a well-defined way. Their existence does not depend on, and is not influenced by, an observer. According to the Newtonian view of reality, we may be confident that everything—the words on this page, an apple, and a puppy—possesses an objective, already-existing reality, a real status independent of anyone or anything else. Participants' questions do not affect them.

The *quantum* game of "Twenty Questions," according to Wheeler, suggests an entirely different idea of reality. The quantum game requires that a person *not* choose a particular object to hold in mind. Instead, he or she replies to participants' questions with yes or no answers that are consistent with one another. The answer yes to the question "Is the object smaller than a shoe?" precludes answering yes to the question "Is the object bigger than an elephant?" As questioning proceeds, the answers increasingly limit the unknown object, making it more and more difficult to give an answer consistent with all the previous replies. Eventually, when the twentieth question is asked, the person answering has no choice but to think of, and name, one particular object.

In the quantum game of "Twenty Questions," unlike the case in the classical version, the object takes on a definite, real identity in the person's mind *only when the final question is asked*. The object does not actually crystallize in the person's thinking until someone asks, "Is it a coffee cup?" At that moment, the person is compelled, given the requirement of consistency, to answer, "Yes." The dependence of the person's object on questions asked by others is analogous to the view of subatomic particles described by quantum physics.

A subatomic particle does not have a definite position until an experiment asks a question that forces it to commit to a definite position.

Quantum physics raises the question, "Did a particle with position X exist before we conducted an experiment to measure its position?"[8] Perhaps we who participate in the universe in some way bring it into being: "The vital act is the act of participation. 'Participator' is the incontrovertible new concept given by quantum mechanics. It strikes down the term 'observer' of classical theory."[9] In effect, our response to Earth's kaleidoscopic beauty helps draw forth that beauty.

The notion that relationships bring about reality has been expressed in another way by saying that the universe is a system of infinitely interrelated systems, from subatomic particles to galaxies. According to this view, science sees "nature itself as . . . a giant system maintaining itself. . . . The solar system and the galaxy of which it is a part are also systems."[10] A system is a distinctive structure made up of the relationships that exist among its parts. Parts are organized and interact in ways that generate a whole that is greater than the sum of its parts. The whole arises from the *interaction* of parts; it differs from the parts. Different from the parts, the whole possesses its own unique qualities. A pile of hydrogen and oxygen atoms that do not interact is not a system. But when the atoms connect in specific ways, they create water, a whole that is markedly different from, and greater than, the sum of its parts.

According to modern physics, then, when we regard the material world, we do not see things as they are. We believe that we see solid matter. But, in fact, everything around us actually consists of minuscule nonvisible "quanta"—quantities of something—dancing in and out of relationships in the empty space of atoms. Relationships are the essence of existence. To be is to be related. If relationships did not bind all things together into systems and subsystems, then we would be unable to communicate, for language depends on connecting parts of speech into intelligible wholes. We would remember nothing, for memory depends on making connections. Severed from our past and from others, we would lose our selves and live in total isolation. *Quantum physics insists that nothing is itself without everything else.* As the poet William Butler Yeats has put it:

O chestnut-tree, great-rooted blossomer,
Are you the leaf, the blossom or the bole?
O body swayed to music, O brightening glance,
How can we know the dancer from the dance?[11]

Summary of Conceptual Highlights of Quantum Theory

- Questions are answered only when asked: Properties of quantum objects do not have definite values prior to a measurement that requires them to choose definite values.
- Interference of possibilities: In quantum theory, if there are different possible ways for any event to happen, then these possibilities can *interfere* with each other. As a result, what we observe when there are two (or more) possible ways for something to happen is *not* just the sum of what we get by considering each of the two possibilities separately.
- Fundamental uncertainty: Quantum theory gives as its final answer only a prediction of *probabilities* for what we will find when we observe something. The theory thus introduces a fundamental *uncertainty* into reality. It never tells you exactly what will happen under given circumstances. You can prepare an experiment the same way every time and yet get different results each time (though usually within a very narrow range of results, according to the probabilities predicted by the theory).
- Entanglement: Things do not always have an isolated identity and isolated properties. Their properties may be defined only in relation to the properties of other things.

THREE UNIVERSAL PRINCIPLES

The new quantum, relational, and systemic view of reality that scientists now posit as an alternative to the Newtonian worldview can be seen as focusing on three principles: interdependence, self-organization, and differentiation.[12] Each of these principles sheds new light on how we practice education.

The Principle of Interdependence

The principle of interdependence refers to the scientific discovery that the entire universe is a system of relationships in which everything is connected inextricably to everything else. This principle describes the systemic nature of the universe. Everything in the universe is simultaneously a system and a subsystem, a part of a larger system. For example, the sun, itself a system, pours forth light as the source of energy that sustains all living things—living systems—on Earth. Modern science invites us to pay close attention to the relationships that exist among all things and to note the complexity that arises from these connections. Indeed, one of the most profound conclusions of modern science is that all things—human and nonhuman, living and nonliving—exist in a delicate pattern of relationships. As Gary Zukav explains in *The Dancing Wu Li Masters,* "All of the things in our universe (including us) that appear to exist independently are actually parts of one all-encompassing organic pattern, and . . . no parts of that pattern are ever really separate from it or from each other."[13]

Such interdependence is observed even at the microlevel of the atom. To understand this, think of an atom as if it were the size of Yankee Stadium. Its nucleus would be smaller than a tiny pebble sitting on the ground in center field. Its outer parts would be the size of tiny gnats buzzing high in the air, higher than a ball could soar. Between the pebble on the ground and the buzzing gnats in the air would be nothing but immense space. So great is the space in an atom that if that space were removed from the atoms in our bodies, each of us would become far smaller than the smallest grain of sand.[14] Despite the apparent vastness of the distance separating the components of atoms—distances that in relative terms rival the distances between stars—all of the trillions of atoms in our bodies function as a coherent system of tightly knit relationships, woven in endless patterns of interdependency that appear to us as human beings.

The Principle of Interdependence and Education

Modern science challenges us to adopt a new worldview as we think about schools and classrooms. Most of us have always viewed reality in Newtonian terms as "out there," something that we can push and control by exerting external pressures. New science insists, however, that reality is shaped by, and emerges from, relationships. The principle of interdependence that weaves all things together reveals that schools are unique wholes composed of relationships among teachers, students, administrators, and all other members of a school and its surrounding community. Just as in nature healthy relationships yield positive results, so in education strong relationships produce excellent schools. Attempts to control people as if they were independent objects working in isolation from one another damage relationships and thus weaken schools. Quality education arises from the school's unique system of relationships. It cannot be achieved in response to externally imposed rules and targets that disrupt this system.

The principle of interdependence tells us that all things are related to one another in systems and subsystems. This principle invites educators to cherish and build relationships. From these respectful, caring relationships will emerge a purposeful school interested in every child. When educators are mindful of the principle of interdependence, they recognize that relationships permeate everything. Accordingly, they make an effort to know every adult and student in the school. They connect with colleagues, interact with students, form partnerships with the community, and collaborate purposefully to achieve a shared understanding of academic excellence. In these ways they help their school offer quality education for all.

The Principle of Self-Organization

The principle of self-organization, or self-creativity, tells us that every living system is unique and can respond to "changing conditions. . . . If natural systems were merely to maintain the status quo throughout the range of circumstances they encounter, there would be no evolution, no patterns of development. . . . Things would either succeed in remaining what they are, or go under."[15] Adjusting to feedback from its environment, the living system can change and grow, yet still retain its original identity. This capacity of natural systems to self-organize is one of the most important general insights of modern science.

Living systems have a remarkable ability to maintain their identity in the face of challenging circumstances. The immune system detects and resolves internal abnormalities, and in so doing it permits the whole living system to maintain its unique self. The living system detects new conditions in its immediate surroundings and adjusts to them while retaining its inner being. As the living system interacts with its environment, new capacities emerge, and yet these new capacities do not alter the system's essential self.

When self-organizing systems interact with their environment, invariably they influence, and are influenced by, other systems. Each system provides inputs for other systems, receives their inputs, and responds to them. Just as two persons building a brick wall affect one another if they are both using the same pile of bricks, so one system's behavior affects the behavior of another system.[16] Living systems compete, but they cooperate much more. They "pollinate each other, create shelter for each other, build firm structures that lift smaller species up to the light . . . pass around nutrients, share territory."[17] In addition, self-organizing systems restrain one another from growing excessively. Earth's living systems say, "Stop, enough. . . . Everything born of the Earth grows to its appropriate size and then stops. . . . Creatures learn, mature, diversify, evolve, create amazing beauty and novelty and complexity, but live within absolute limits."[18]

The dynamic response of self-organizing systems to feedback from their environment resembles our notion of awareness. For example, the single-celled organism acts as if it were aware of the world outside its membrane. It avoids harmful things such as acid and gravitates to whatever seems beneficial, such as a sugar solution. The deer notices predators. Even the deer's immune system has its own response, reminiscent of awareness, as it notices hostile interlopers and alerts the body to fight illness. According to biologist Lynn Margulis, "Everything in the universe has consciousness—some kind of awareness. . . . [This awareness] is a private affair. It is not directly measurable. But an inability to render a quality measurable is no reason to assume its absence."[19] *Awareness* in this sense describes the sensitivity that plants experience in response to sunlight and temperature changes. Plants perceive and react to their surroundings, as do other living systems, even though they do not have a human being's ability to reflect on their perceptions and sensitivities.

A living system's ability to perceive and react to its environment underscores its uniqueness and latent potentiality. Every living system is a distinctive entity, and as such it contains the potential to change and grow while still maintaining its essential self. Its full potential emerges gradually as it reacts to circumstances. Any human being's potential, for example, is drawn into existence by each day's crises and opportunities. *Until daily life summons you to act,* "you do not know what you can do, or who you are in your fullest significance, or what powers are hiding within you."[20]

Were the capacity for self-organization to vanish, then surely latent potential and uniqueness would cease to exist. Nothing would grow or develop. Humans would always behave in the same way. They would be devoid of new insights and trapped in routine. Lacking awareness, plants and animals would sicken and die. The sun would not flare forth, realizing its latent potential to illuminate the Earth, and the Earth would turn to dust.[21]

The Principle of Self-Organization and Education

What does it matter for education that modern science gives us insight into the principle of self-organization? This insight encourages everyone who cares about education to think in a new way about teaching and learning. People who regard schools as self-organizing systems will nurture a school's uniqueness and latent potential. They will seek ways to help large inner-city schools change and improve in response to their harsh environment. They will also recognize when rural schools are well suited to their circumstances and help them continue to flourish. Teachers who adopt the principle of self-organization will focus on each child's unique talents and interests. They will give students a wide variety of opportunities to develop their distinctive abilities and sharpen their minds. Teachers who understand self-organization will arrange for many kinds of continuous feedback that make it possible to interpret each child's progress on the pathway to academic excellence. These teachers will know that only by taking an active interest in their individual students can they ignite enthusiasm for learning. Humberto Maturana, the great Chilean neuroscientist, says that "if you want autonomous and coherent behavior, you need only open a space of love, and intelligence appears there."[22]

Acting in harmony with the principle of self-organization that pervades all living systems, educators not only will help students but also will help themselves. These educators will do the things they say students should do. They will become the kinds of people they want students to become, and they will treat colleagues in ways that draw forth the other person's fullness of being as well as their own.

A self-organizing school regards itself as inextricably connected to, not separate from, the local community. The principle of self-organization reminds educators that it is necessary for schools, parents, and local community members to maintain respectful and dynamic relationships. These relationships can give schools important information about how well schools are serving their needs.

The principle of self-organization, which attributes change and growth in large part to information received from the environment, reveals that traditional public schools do have the potential to become quality schools. From weaving new patterns and forming new relationships, traditional public schools can draw forth their own potential to create pathways to excellence for every young person.

Educators acting in harmony with the principle of self-organization know every student and each student's individual circumstances. They believe in each young person's capacity to excel. They see every student as unique, full of promise, and capable of taking action to create the self. They also recognize that self-organization requires freedom to make choices. Traditional public schools are free when teachers choose the methods and materials they know will enable them to teach effectively. Traditional public schools are free when superintendents and principals encourage and sustain relationships within the school and between the school and the community. Nurturing these relationships and allowing them to flourish generate the rich learning environment necessary to draw forth the full promise of every child.

The Principle of Differentiation

Modern science has made discoveries that call attention to a principle of differentiation at work throughout the universe. Because of this principle of differentiation, kangaroos, squirrels, whales, and sparrows keep us company on this planet, along with at least thirty million other species. The principle of differentiation is inextricably joined to the principles of interdependence and self-organization. Everything in the universe is related to everything else, according to the principle of interdependence. These relationships draw forth every entity's potential, according to the principle of self-organization. The principle of differentiation tells us that the universe perpetually creates infinite diversity. From simple means—a few basic properties and a few simple rules—the universe generates ever-increasing complexity.

Working in fields that had been widely separated in the past, modern scientists have made discoveries that lead to startling inferences. Their achievements suggest that all the variety and complexity on Earth result from the constant application of a few simple rules to a few basic properties: "All organisms are composed of basically the same substances . . . cells, composed of molecules, and molecules composed of atoms of carbon, hydrogen, oxygen, nitrogen, iodine, phosphorus, potassium, sulfur, calcium, sodium, chlorine, iron, and a few others; the difference between Caesar and the chimp is not primarily a difference in substance but in the relational structuring of the substances."[23] The difference between a computer keyboard and the skin on the typist's hands cannot be explained by their parts. The electrons in both are identical, so that if they were exchanged, it would be impossible to tell the difference. The difference between the keyboard and the typist's skin arises because basic rules have been applied in distinctive ways to produce unique combinations of basic substances.

The power of a few rules to generate complexity is illustrated by the game of chess. In chess, a few rules restrict the movements of the chess pieces, yet these few rules can be applied in seemingly inexhaustible ways to yield an astonishing array of possible scenarios.[24] In nature a few rules are applied in infinite ways to produce the combinations of basic "stuff" that yield Earth's magnificent diversity.

The principle of differentiation encompasses the complex movement from simple means—the application of a few abiding rules and the use of a few immutable properties—to immense variety and unfathomable complexity. This movement toward complexity is evident in symbiosis, an arrangement whereby two different types of live beings coexist together intimately and depend on one another for survival. Dependent on one another as they are, these beings are no longer single but, rather, a composite unit. Together they create a complex whole that allows both to thrive. The human intestine, for example, provides a home for bacteria, and the bacteria produce vitamins that benefit the human body. Differentiation also enables two nonliving entities to produce a third, such as when hydrogen and oxygen merge to create water.[25]

Because of the principle of differentiation, the planet is robust. Differentiation makes for strength, whereas sameness weakens and imperils. Were the principle of differentiation to cease operating, music would be one note, artists would paint the same subjects using the same techniques, poets would use identical imagery, and sameness would flatten life into a bleak, gray wasteland. The universe would be a homogeneous blob, fragile and poised for collapse.

The Principle of Differentiation and Education

The principle of differentiation shows us that Earth is always producing rich ends from simple means, continuously generating diversity. The simple means—the same basic rules applied in endless variation to the same fundamental building blocks—lead to stunningly diverse systems, living and nonliving. With the discovery of the principle of differentiation, modern science calls on educators to draw forth their students' creativity. Mindful of this principle, educators encourage young people to create, to acquire knowledge and develop skills through self-directed active learning, and to enrich their lives by embracing diversity. They teach them to delight in the cascade of variety that gives fullness to life.

Teaching in the light of this principle involves asking students to imagine, experiment, investigate, and question. It involves using a variety of learning styles and encouraging young people to proceed at their own rate. Mindful of life's generous diversity, educators are suspicious of the narrow assumption that the only right ambition is to get a well-paying job in a prestigious occupation. Consequently, they help young people discover their true interests and find the callings that make them happy.

THE NEW WORLDVIEW SAYS "MANAGE THE MEANS"

Modern science has made discoveries that give us a new worldview, a new way to think about and to understand experience now, in this present moment. The new science suggests that three principles permeate the universe, sustaining all natural systems. These universal principles of interdependence, self-organization, and differentiation provide a new model for education in the twenty-first century. Were these principles applied consistently to education, together they would help transform traditional public schools into places of limitless possibility.

These principles focus on the life-sustaining relationships, activity, and potential of natural systems. They indicate that attention to the day's circumstances produces the aims of education. Anything that nurtures the means, that is, anything that nurtures the school, its relationships, its students, and its daily affairs, contributes to a quality academic education for every child and a common culture for the good of a democratic society.

NOTES

1. Thomas Berry, *The Great Work: Our Way into the Future* (New York: Bell Tower, 1999), 23–43; Frijof Capra, *The Turning Point: Science, Society, and the Rising Culture* (New York: Bantam Books, 1988); 75–97; Eric J. Chaisson, *Cosmic Evolution: The Rise of Complexity in Nature* (Cambridge: Harvard University Press, 2001), 1–41; Brian Swimme and Thomas Berry, *The Universe Story: From the Primordial Flaring Forth to the Ecozoic Era* (San Francisco: HarperSanFrancisco, 1992), 12–44.

2. Molly Brown and Joanna Macy, "Teaching Sustainability: Whole Systems Learning," unpublished MS, 11 October 2002, 1–12.

3. Gary Zukav, *The Dancing Wu Li Masters: An Overview of the New Physics* (New York: William Morrow, 1979), 55. See also Capra, *The Turning Point;* and Frijof Capra, *The Web of Life: A New Scientific Understanding of Living Systems* (New York: Anchor, 1996).

4. Zukav, *The Dancing Wu Li Masters,* 21–32, 46, 54–62; Brian Swimme, *The Hidden Heart of the Cosmos: Humanity and the New Story* (Maryknoll, N.Y.: Orbis Books, 1999), 55–62; Brian Swimme (performer), *The Fundamental Order of the Cosmos* (Mill Valley, Calif.: New Story Project Video, 1990 [video]).

5. Todd L. Duncan, "Guidance from Nature," unpublished MS, 19 March 2003; see also Todd L. Duncan, *An Ordinary World: The Role of Science in Your Search for Personal Meaning* (Hillsboro, Oreg.: Science Integration Institute, 2001).

6. Zukav, *The Dancing Wu Li Masters*, 57.

7. John A. Wheeler, "Information, Physics, Quantum: The Search for Links," in *Complexity, Entropy and the Physics of Information*, ed. Wojciech H. Zurek (Cambridge, Mass.: Perseus Publishing, 1990), 11.

8. Zukav, *The Dancing Wu Li Masters*, 54.

9. John A. Wheeler, K. S. Thorne, and C. Misner, *Gravitation* (San Francisco: Freeman, 1973), 1273.

10. Ervin Lazlo, *The Systems View of the World* (New York: George Braziller, 1972), 11, 27–34.

11. William Butler Yeats, "Among School Children," in *The Collected Poems of W. B. Yeats* (New York: Macmillan Publishing Co., 1956), 212.

12. Swimme and Berry, *The Universe Story*, 12–44, 71–79.

13. Zukav, *The Dancing Wu Li Masters*, 73

14. Brian Swimme, *The Universe Is a Green Dragon: A Cosmic Creation Story* (Santa Fe: Bear and Co. Publishing, 1984), 37–38; Zukav, *The Dancing Wu Li Masters*, 73.

15. Brown and Macy, *Teaching Sustainability*, 10; Duncan, *An Ordinary World*, 9–11; Swimme, *The Universe Is a Green Dragon*; Zukav, *The Dancing Wu Li Masters*.

16. Lazlo, *The Systems View of the World*, 46–49.

17. Donella Meadows, "Economics Laws Clash with Planet's," *Timeline*, no. 57 (May-June 2001): 8–9.

18. Meadows, "Economics Laws Clash with Planet's," 8.

19. Lynn Margulis and Dorian Sagan, *What Is Life?* (New York: Simon and Schuster, 1995), 122.

20. Swimme, *The Universe Is a Green Dragon*, 51; Lazlo, *The Systems View of the World*, 87–88.

21. Swimme and Berry, *The Universe Story*, 72–73; Swimme, *The Universe Is a Green Dragon*, 47–52.

22. Humberto Maturana and Pille Bunnell, "The Biology of Business: Love Expands Intelligence," *Reflections: The SoL Journal* 1, no. 2 (winter 1999): 61–62.

23. Lazlo, *The Systems View of the World*, 32; Duncan, *An Ordinary World*, 8–15.

24. Duncan, *An Ordinary World*, 8–15.

25. Margulis and Sagan, *What Is Life?* 96.

CHAPTER 4

Improving Your Child's Public School

Science, not business, gives us ideas that can help us improve America's traditional single public school system. Modern science reveals that everything in the universe is related to everything else. Every living system is connected to, and depends on, others. But business tells schools, themselves living systems, to be autonomous and to compete as if they were divorced from society's larger educational enterprise. Modern science reveals that all natural systems are self-organizing. As self-organizing entities, they react spontaneously to their environment, and their free response lets them develop their full potential. But business offers schools top-down management that stifles spontaneity by controlling behavior with rewards and punishments. Modern science reveals that differentiation characterizes the universe. Natural systems drive to generate new systems; they drive to generate diversity. But business wants schools to aim at measurable targets—standardized achievement test scores—even though focusing on test scores inhibits creativity and lessens diversity. America's traditional system of public education can serve the country well if policy makers, business leaders, and educators look to science for new ideas rather than to business.

Richard F. Elmore, the Anrig Professor of Educational Leadership at the Harvard Graduate School of Education, points out that an "atomized, fragmented, incoherent school" can be transformed into a coherent and effective school under the right conditions.[1] This book contends that when a school's interior condition reflects the principles of interrelatedness, self-organization, and differentiation that scientists observe in living systems, that school will improve. These principles are implicit in schools that possess a common purpose, a unified culture, wise leaders, parental involvement, capable teachers who connect with others, and community support. Such schools, because they operate the way that natural systems work, achieve significant and lasting improvements. These improvements occur because—whether or not members of a school realize it—their actions correspond to the universal principles that guide natural systems.

Unfortunately, just as living systems often suffer from an inhospitable environment, so schools obviously suffer when their environment—whether local, state, or federal—deprives them of necessary resources. In cases where the public adamantly refuses to give adequate financial support to schools, the efforts of principals and teachers to deliver quality education are severely hampered.

MONEY MAKES THE DIFFERENCE

Apparently, a great many Americans are no longer willing to fund public schools. They reject the belief that has been accepted by the general public since the mid-nineteenth century—namely, that all adults, whether parents or not, rightfully pay for public education because educated citizens benefit the whole society. And yet this argument still holds true. The nation's citizens must be educated—the talented and gifted, those learning English as a second language, students from fractured homes, those suffering from abuse and neglect, those labeled "learning disabled," and all the other young people in this country. Yet without adequate funding, traditional public schools cannot educate the immensely diverse students who depend on them. Surprisingly, to many this fact is not self-evident. Not only are Americans increasingly unwilling to spend money on public education, but also they actually believe that doing so is futile.

Critics of school funding argue that money does not improve schools. They claim that there is absolutely no correlation between expenditure per pupil and student test scores. Critics are right to insist that merely spending money on a public school will not solve that school's problems. Money alone is not a *sufficient* cause to transform a school. However, adequate funding is undeniably a necessary *contributing* cause. It takes funding for schools to self-organize in response to student and community needs. It takes funding to hire teachers, break massive schools into small ones, divide huge classes into small classes, replace worn-out equipment and old textbooks, renovate decrepit buildings, offer rich academic and extracurricular programs, make available diverse learning opportunities, and serve the pressing needs of young people.

From rural areas in Montana to urban high schools in Baltimore, countless children rely on schools for safety, food, positive relationships with caring adults, and even medical help. A teacher in rural Alaska says of her high school students, "These kids have already shut down when they walk in the room. They are poor, neglected, and defeated. We take them as they come and try to help them turn around again. If I get a glimmer of interest for a minute, I'm excited, but usually kids are tuned out. The school can't pay for the kind of activities I would like to use to grab kids. If I can make them want to learn, though, there's a point to what I do."[2]

The barren home life of low-income students all over the nation drastically affects their academic performance: "Differences in test scores, grades, and other measures between affluent white students and low income students of color . . . are [caused] not so much [by] race as [by] class."[3] Although student achievement is dramatically influenced by a child's living conditions, poverty and neglect do not have to condemn students to failure. If rural and urban schools were properly financed, then they would be able to give students the individual attention and exciting learning opportunities that motivate them to do their best. After all, children in the suburbs, where high property taxes generously fund schools, typically do well academically. Surely their success occurs in large part because they attend pleasant facilities, study current textbooks, use good equipment, and attend small classes.[4] Inner-city schoolchildren, however, are forced to occupy decaying facilities, use out-of-date textbooks, struggle with damaged equipment, get ignored in huge classes, are seldom exposed to music and art, and rarely go on field trips. No wonder they have trouble reaching high academic standards.

So widespread is the inequity between poor rural and inner-city schools and suburban schools that lawsuits have been filed in forty-four states to equalize school funding. Court rulings in about half of these states have directed state legislatures to increase funding to poor schools. For example, in 1989 the Kentucky Supreme Court ordered the state to create a new structure to treat Appalachian districts fairly. The Ohio Supreme Court ruled that Ohio's educational system was unconstitutional and ordered the state to spend $1 billion to fix it. Maryland's low-income schools so urgently need improvement that Maryland proposes to increase spending on education to 75 percent more than its present level by the year 2008.[5]

It may be true that money alone cannot guarantee that a school will provide an excellent education. It is possible, certainly, that money might be misused. But without money, the plans and strategies of even the most enlightened principal and faculty will be unable to revive a declining school. Let us consider the plans and actions that make it possible for schools to use funds effectively to achieve desirable aims.

A SUCCESS STORY

Just as the parts of any living system exist in relation to one another, and these relationships produce a unique whole that is different from the sum of its parts, so members of a school are interrelated. They form connections and weave patterns that produce a school's distinctive culture. To offer children a quality education, all members of a school need to relate to one another in pursuit of clear aims. Research shows that when school employees collaborate to develop and share the same explicit expectations about what happens in a good school, *together they will make a good school*. The "beliefs, norms, expectations, and practices that all people in an organization share . . . [dictate] the ability of a school to make improvements."[6] Secretaries, cooks, custodians, bus drivers, assistant principals, mentors, interns, teachers, and the principal must collaborate to describe their school's purpose. They must agree on the contribution each of them will make to attain this purpose.

Sharing a common purpose enables all staff members to relate to one another and to students in constructive ways that promote high academic standards. The remarkable success story of Bemiss Elementary

School in Spokane, Washington, illustrates this point. On 28 February 1993 an article in Spokane's newspaper, *The Spokesman Review,* stated that Bemiss Elementary School "holds the distinction of being the district's lowest scoring school [on the state's standardized achievement test]."[7] The newspaper did not mention that 85 percent of the children attending this K–6 school live in poverty and that 20 percent of the children do not speak English.

Although the humiliating newspaper story embarrassed the entire staff at Bemiss Elementary, they did not waste time defending themselves by offering excuses for their students' low performance. Instead, every employee in the school viewed the headline as a direct challenge and resolved that in the future every young person at Bemiss Elementary would reach high academic standards. Academic excellence, not earning high test scores, became their goal. By 2002 Bemiss Elementary School had progressed from having the lowest rating in the State of Washington, as determined by standardized achievement test scores, to earning the equivalent of a B rating. It received an award honoring its distinguished improvement. How was this improvement accomplished? Every step taken, although not by design, harmonized with the three principles suggested by modern science.

All members of the school collaborated first to figure out practices that would improve teaching and increase learning. Meeting often and regularly, they decided exactly what actions would strengthen Bemiss for the children's sake. Emerging from these meetings was the clear understanding, first, that the purpose of Bemiss Elementary School is to free its children from poverty and, second, that academic knowledge alone provides escape from poverty. It then became the task of every person in the school to help Bemiss children learn the academic content stipulated in Washington State's official content standards. Everyone in the school had a role to play that helped children master academic subjects. All staff members carried a card on which was written Bemiss Elementary School's mission statement: "Our mission is to be a caring community of learners (staff, parents, students) where all students learn the necessary academic and social skills and abilities to be able to make choices in their lives."[8]

Having formulated a mission, Bemiss Elementary School staff members next aggressively evaluated the various components of instruction in their school—technology, parent involvement, teaching methods, assessment, early intervention, inclusion, and student issues. Then they formed "action teams" to research each of these components. Their intent was to discover for each element the best practices that Bemiss Elementary School might possibly adopt. Action teams collaborated, sharing their respective research findings. They learned, among other things, that in all grades children need a common vocabulary, clear objectives, and instruction across the curriculum. Writing must be explicitly taught, for instance, in every class. They learned that *the system puts children at risk by not meeting their needs,* and they set about to design a coherent system that would treat each child as a worthy individual capable of succeeding. Realizing that it would take money to introduce the best practices they had discovered, these action teams, having collaborated to design a school-wide improvement plan, sought funding to implement this plan.

A Title I grant enabled Bemiss Elementary School to introduce many effective practices. A central focus was on strengthening teaching. Because, as Bemiss Elementary Principal Lorna L. Spear says, "a teacher's weakness becomes a student's weakness," teachers were given many opportunities to deepen their knowledge and acquire new skills.[9] Turning schools around "entails improving the knowledge and skills of teachers—changing their knowledge of content and how to teach it—and helping them to understand where their students are in their academic performance."[10] To this end, Bemiss Elementary School used grant money to hire four full-time master teachers whose job it was to coach the faculty. These four coaches helped teachers refine, alter, and, in some cases, change entirely the way they taught. Funding also permitted Bemiss to send three teams of four teachers each on several occasions to the Denver Institute for Reading, where they gained specific information about the difficult art of teaching children to read. In addition, the school hired an aide fluent in both Russian and English. This aide interpreted the teacher's remarks for Russian speakers in the class. Bemiss Elementary School discovered that bilingual instruction accelerated the children's mastery of every subject, including English. The faculty learned that when children grasp in their first language the concepts presented in mathematics, reading, and writing classes, they progress quickly.

The experience of Bemiss Elementary School demonstrates that unsatisfactory traditional public schools can be transformed into excellent schools when members form respectful, collaborative relationships that give rise to a shared purpose. Traditional public schools can be improved remarkably when polarized ideologies, competing educational theories, conflicting teaching strategies, and dissension are replaced by interrelatedness, self-organization, and differentiation. Interrelatedness yields coherence. Self-organization, as opposed to top-down control, yields changes appropriate to the needs of the community. Regard for diversity calls on a school and its community to draw forth the full promise of every child.

WISE LEADERSHIP ACCORDING TO THE PRINCIPLES OF MODERN SCIENCE

Lorna Spear's success at Bemiss Elementary illustrates the influence of a wise leader. Wise leadership occurs when the leader's habits of thought are consistent, consciously or unconsciously, with the new worldview of modern science. Intuitively or intentionally, wise leaders act in ways that nurture interrelatedness, self-organization, and differentiation. They are strong enough to provide direction and yet wise enough to rely on the distinctive contributions of every member of their staff. They recognize, furthermore, that "students are not 'at risk,' they are 'at promise,' and that only the system puts them at risk."[11]

Superintendents improve schools when they know well and understand the system, the inner workings, of each school in their district. Rather than impose top-down mandates that risk disrupting a school's culture, twenty-first-century superintendents acquire firsthand knowledge of a school's academic content, standards, and teaching practices. They give principals freedom to act in ways that generate excellence.

Principals improve schools when they know how to direct, support, persuade, and nurture staff and students. Principals succeed when they facilitate school-wide conversations that lead to a common purpose. Lorna Spear, the principal of Bemiss Elementary School, for example, met often with staff members to give all employees the opportunity to weave themselves into a harmonious community dedicated to a common goal. Familiar with the interests and talents of every staff member, Spear delegated responsibility to a willing staff. She also worked creatively with the parents and community at large, encouraging their participation in the children's education.

Creating and sustaining a coherent, purposeful school system is perhaps a principal's most significant achievement. To bring coherence, structure, and purpose to a school and to motivate people to weave a web of relationships that unites everyone to serve the children require habits of thought alien to those featured in MBA programs and typical programs for educational administrators. A wise educational leader is not comparable to a CEO who sacrifices people to achieve quantitative targets. Wise leadership harmonizes with the principles of modern science.

Leadership and the Principle of Interrelatedness

The principle of interrelatedness expresses the scientific discovery that everything in the universe is interdependent and interconnected. Everything—human and nonhuman, living and nonliving—is related to everything else. Everything participates in a delicate pattern, an intricate web of relationships. This principle requires that leaders see students, teachers, cooks, gardeners, janitors, secretaries, bus drivers, parents, community partners, mentors, and interns as important contributors to the richness of the school's culture and to the well-being of each student.[12] The following list highlights particular steps that leaders can take to reinforce the idea of interrelatedness:

1. Twenty-first-century leaders who are guided by the principle of interrelatedness *make connections:*
   - They strive to nurture relationships.
   - They reach out to students, faculty, and all other members of their school and community.
   - They consistently promote linking academic subjects and connecting classrooms to the community.
   - They trust the intelligence of those whose lives they influence.
   - They confer regularly with faculty and parents.

2. Twenty-first-century leaders guided by the principle of interrelatedness *collaborate:*
   - They invite faculty to share with one another strategies that are effective in their classrooms and programs.
   - They encourage faculty members to test new ideas, to discuss these experiments with colleagues, and to move ahead to learn more.
   - They promote student involvement in collaborative learning enterprises.
   - They form partnerships with community members and business leaders.
   - They ask the local community and school personnel their vision of the school's future.
3. Twenty-first-century leaders guided by the principle of interrelatedness *attend to process and detail:*
   - They know each student's circumstances.
   - They are mindful of the specific problems, strengths, and potential of every faculty member.
   - They meet with parents.
   - They recognize that teachers, students, parents, community members, and those in business are part of and contribute to the processes—the means, the web of interrelated details—that result in a desired end.
   - They pay close attention to the web of details, the elements of the process, from which desired ends emerge.
   - They participate in myriad ways, such as visiting classrooms, the cafeteria, the music room, and the school store and attending student presentations of class projects, student plays, and athletic events.

Leadership and the Principle of Self-Organization

The principle of self-organization holds that every living system is unique and able to self-organize—to change and adapt while preserving its essential self—in response to its environment. The living system adapts to feedback from its environment, adjusting and changing to maintain its essential self. The "self" achieves order, balance, and direction. The self, the inner being, of every living system is *latent potential* that emerges in the process of doing daily life. Leaders who know this principle will pursue the following steps, and more, to make it possible for their schools to give everyone's latent potential the chance to cascade into being:[13]

1. Twenty-first-century leaders who are guided by the principle of self-organization *respect and draw forth everyone's potential:*
   - They draw forth their own potential as they grow intellectually, personally, and spiritually.
   - They understand and support the human need to find meaning in daily life.
   - They create opportunities for faculty to increase their knowledge and skills.
   - They build an environment that motivates all students to do their best.
   - They help community members recognize their full potential as partners in education.
2. Twenty-first-century leaders guided by the principle of self-organization *promote critical thinking:*
   - They think systematically about their own thinking processes to achieve the fullest understanding possible.
   - They welcome unfamiliar points of view, accept sound evidence, and examine assumptions in the light of new information.
   - They provide opportunities for faculty to study critical and creative thinking.
   - They seek ways to include critical and creative thinking across the curriculum.
3. Twenty-first-century leaders guided by the principle of self-organization *inspire hope:*
   - They present opportunities for staff and students to understand and cultivate emotional intelligence.
   - They are positive.
   - They acknowledge the inevitability of their own and others' mistakes and take them in stride, neither casting blame nor accepting failure.

- They celebrate minor and major student, faculty, and school achievements.
- They offer unflagging support and encouragement.

Leadership and the Principle of Differentiation

The principle of differentiation refers to nature's infinite creativity and ceaseless drive to produce infinite variety, abundance, and uniqueness. Nature never repeats itself. Because of the principle of differentiation, one star cannot stand for all stars any more than one person can stand for all persons. Modern leaders, aware of this principle, savor and encourage creativity, variety, and diversity in all the following ways:[14]

1. Twenty-first-century leaders who are guided by the principle of differentiation *appreciate and admire differences and uniqueness:*
   - They respect uniqueness, admire differences, and know the ethnic, social, economic, and religious backgrounds of those in their school and community.
   - They promote active, student-centered learning that develops each child's unique abilities.
   - They encourage the many interests and talents of students and faculty.
   - They recognize that diverse learning styles require a variety of teaching methods.
   - They generate a context that lets students learn in their own way and at their own pace.
2. Twenty-first-century leaders guided by the principle of differentiation *prize creativity:*
   - They encourage a culture that admires each student's interests, talents, and learning style.
   - They celebrate those who imagine, experiment, and try new ideas.
   - They encourage creativity by supporting study of the fine and performing arts.
   - They seek fresh ideas and are open to new possibilities.
   - They ask if routine practices are still viable.
   - They examine their own and other people's assumptions.
   - They ask difficult and probing questions.

A wise leader is a school's defense against discouragement, apathy, coercion, contentiousness, and frustration. A wise leader challenges a school to make its best effort to become an excellent learning organization, despite pressures that militate against academic excellence. Just as wise leaders are necessary to a school's improvement, so are supportive relationships between the school and the community it serves.

INVOLVING PARENTS AND THE COMMUNITY

Schools improve when they are connected to their community and enjoy parental support. Unfortunately, the bond of mutual understanding between parents and educators began to deteriorate beginning in the late 1950s with the proliferation of immense, factorylike, impersonal middle schools and high schools. The bleak immensity of these schools designed to hold from 1,000 to 2,000 students not only condemns students to loneliness and isolates teachers but also intimidates parents. Parents turn silently away from massive schools. Nor are they always willing to visit small schools. A chronic disconnect between parents and educators means that a great many schools are isolated from the families and communities they are supposed to benefit. Isolated schools that operate in a vacuum cannot fulfill their community's needs. A school, although a system, is also a subsystem of its larger community. As part of the larger whole, its task is to form relationships with parents and community members. From these relationships comes a whole social system resolved to leave no child behind.

Mindful that education is everyone's concern, Bemiss Elementary School in Washington State holds several events for parents such as family nights and kindergarten literacy lunches. It holds a number of events because parents who cannot attend one may be able to attend another. Susan B. Anthony Elementary School in Sacramento, California, aggressively reaches out to parents. Most students attending this school live in poverty. All of them receive free or reduced-price lunches, and 76 percent of them are learning English as their second language. Despite the disadvantages these children face, they are managing to reach California State's academic standards. One reason for their success is the Home Visit Project that links parents, teachers, and counselors. Principal Carol Sharp's assistant has explained that because working parents found it hard to come to the school building, the Home Visit Project was devised to enable Susan B. Anthony's teachers and counselors to routinely visit their students' homes. Two staff members, at least one of whom is bilingual, visit a student's home. The first of these visits, all of which are designed to weave a strong connection between family and school, focuses on the parents' dreams for their child and on what parents think the school community, especially teachers, might do to help their child improve. As a result of these visits, parents and educators have formed relationships that have made a positive difference for children. Grades are going up, and suspensions have been greatly reduced.[15]

Unless a school communicates well with parents and other members of its community, it cannot respond intelligently to community concerns. Frequent and open communication between school and community can avert offenses that erode parents' confidence in a school. For example, suppose that many community members embrace a religion that deplores Halloween. If a principal realizes that parents intend to keep their children home from school rather than expose them to a Halloween celebration, the principal is then in a position to decide that educating the children takes precedence over holding Halloween festivities. The principal is in a position to honor the community by canceling the school's Halloween activities.[16]

A school exists to serve the community's children, and it can only serve these children if families trust the schools. Regular conversations between school staff and community members are necessary to generate the trust that comes from mutual understanding.

TEACHERS MAKE ALL THE DIFFERENCE

Close relationships among schools, parents, and the community contribute greatly to a school's improvement. Of course, excellent teaching is absolutely indispensable to improvement. Only knowledgeable, skilled, and caring teachers can make a school known for delivering quality education.

Teachers change young people's lives for better or worse. Most of us can name at least one teacher who helped us find our way and probably one who let us down. Teachers understand the profound effect they have on young people, and most of them do their best, sometimes in a harsh environment, to draw forth the potential of each one of their students. Because our society depends on the skill and expertise of its teachers, it is curious that so many people regard teachers in a condescending light. In America, however, unlike other industrialized nations, "teacher bashing" seems to be gaining in popularity. Critics fault teachers for not working hard enough, not knowing their material, not being skilled at communicating lessons, and not caring about students.

Believing, apparently, that many of the nation's teachers are either indifferent or incompetent, the general public seeks accountability and finds it in standardized achievement test scores. But, certainly, teachers have always been held accountable. That is, they have always been evaluated, appraised, and directed in many ways. They are accountable every day to students and their parents; to their colleagues, who know what happens in their classrooms; to the principal, superintendent, and school boards that supervise them; to community members who judge their behavior in public; and to the employers, community colleges, and universities that judge their students to be either informed and capable or lacking in knowledge and skill. The school and the community at large, particularly students and their families, know if teachers love their subject, convey it effectively, and show each young person the steps necessary to achieve mastery. Teachers live in a fish bowl; everyone can see whether or not their students are improving.

In addition to constant scrutiny, other conditions complicate the life of professional educators. For example, few avenues for career advancement are available to them, they are often excluded from shaping the policies that affect them, and rules and regulations limit their freedom.[17] Furthermore, it is common knowledge that teachers in the United States spend hundreds more hours in the classroom than do their counterparts in other countries. Consequently, they have little time to work closely with individual students or to discuss subject matter and instructional methods with colleagues.

Although the profession has many drawbacks, nevertheless, teaching attracts bright and dedicated professionals who love their subject and genuinely care about their students. They teach for joy, not for advancement, a big salary, or prestige. Were policy makers and the general public to visit classrooms, talk to schoolteachers, and heed their advice, they would learn quickly about specific actions that would help traditional public schools offer a quality education to every child. Teachers are mindful of problems in their schools and are able to suggest remedies for them. Teachers can help improve schools if they are invited to share their profound experience and keen insights with policy makers, business roundtables, and parents. As it is, often impeded rather than aided by top-down policy decisions, nevertheless, a great many faculty members deliver quality instruction.

From preschool through university, faculty members teach in ways that inspire young people with their own love of a subject and a sense of the importance of knowing it. Filling students with confidence that they, too, can master this subject, teachers put joy in learning. Their instruction does not rely on the mind-numbing memorizing and reciting that filled the school day in the nineteenth and early twentieth centuries, as David Tyack reminds us. Tyack, an eminent education historian, says that in those days "the standardized method of teaching in most urban schools was quite literally to 'toe the line.' That is, the children were expected to come up front and recite to the teacher and stand with their toes lined up to the board and their hands in a particular place as they recited their lesson."[18] Resisting the pressure of standardized achievement tests to turn classes into exercises in memorization, good teachers seriously and respectfully lead discussions on all sides of any issue. Instead of dogmatically pronouncing something to be right or wrong, they receive passionately held views with respect. Forgetful of the self, they walk the path their students walk, offering hope and encouragement.[19]

Adopting teachers as role models, students take to heart what teachers say and often imitate what they do. Innumerable adults are indebted to teachers for contributing to the personal foundations on which they stand. Teachers influence the adult a student will become.[20]

By believing in students, by treating them as if they are intelligent and capable, teachers actually help young people increase their intelligence. When teachers believe that students can learn difficult material, their students catch this belief, act on it, and succeed. The positive effect of a teacher's encouragement has been verified by experiments originating in the 1960s that show that "when teachers were led to believe that their students had extraordinary intellectual potential, these average students really did end up achieving impressively in their classes."[21]

Teachers who use a variety of instructional techniques provide many opportunities for young people to grow intellectually. Because human beings possess multiple intelligences, a range of teaching methods is necessary to facilitate learning.[22] Children learn, for example, when they hear an explanation, see a photograph, organize and arrange objects, inquire, solve problems, build projects, give performances, repeat and practice material, and connect a lesson to their own knowledge and experience. First graders learn mathematics, for instance, when they talk in class about a specific mathematics problem. Vocalizing their thinking helps them clarify the problem they are being asked to solve. They learn when they work together to figure out answers and when they write down the method they used to solve a math problem.

Children who write for a reason write carefully because the work matters. Students always do their best on schoolwork that is done for a significant reason, because it holds meaning. When students see meaning in their work, they pay attention and try to do well. No subject, of course, is intrinsically meaningful. It is assigned meaning by the human brain. The brain, indefatigable in its quest for meaning, constructs meaning when it connects new information with facts and events already stored in the long-term memory.[23] The importance of making these connections is discussed in chapters dealing with teaching mathematics, science, and foreign languages.

In addition to helping students discover meaning by using a variety of teaching methods, teachers improve student performance by employing continuous classroom assessment. Continuous assessment tells teachers exactly what each student is learning. One high school biology instructor assesses student learning by reserving a few minutes at the end of each class for students to write down two questions or comments about something they have not understood. As they leave the classroom, students place their comments in a box next to the door. The instructor begins the next class by addressing the issues commented on by most students. To help students assess their own progress, many teachers hand out written descriptions of what students should know and be able to do as a result of completing specific assignments. They make certain that these objectives reflect the state's academic goals, known as content standards, for each class and grade level. To help students meet course objectives, teachers develop scoring guides that describe the various levels of proficiency from poor to excellent. Students are then able to use scoring guides to rate their own degree of mastery. Students rate themselves at Bemiss Elementary School, for example, using the Hamburger Rubric invented by one of their teachers (see figure 4.1).

4 Deluxe Burger
You have exceeded the basic expectations!
- Stated facts from the problem
- Named the strategy used to solve the problem
- Explained your thinking and showed understanding
- Answered the question being asked
- Very neat and organized

3 Hamburger
You have met the standard!
- Stated facts from the problem
- Named the strategy used to solve the problem
- Explained the steps used to solve the problem
- Answered the question being asked
- Very neat and organized

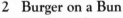

2 Burger on a Bun
You're almost there!
- Your steps are unclear
- Question is partially answered
- Needs more detail

1 Bun
You did not understand
- Work is hard to follow
- Answer does not match question

Figure 4.1. *Student Self-Assessment Source: Principal Lorna Spear, Bemiss Elementary School, Spokane.*

SOCIETY'S GREAT RESPONSIBILITY: IMPROVING TRADITIONAL PUBLIC SCHOOLS

Traditional public schools can be transformed into places that offer all students a quality education. Schools improve when funding provides a warm, nurturing environment that is at once attractive, comfortable, and safe. Schools improve when staff members share a common sense of purpose and collaborate to achieve it. They improve when wise principals and superintendents, thinking in ways that correspond to nature's principles of interdependence, self-organization, and diversity, seek the advice of all school employees and act consistently to support their shared vision. Schools improve when teachers aim at high standards, expect proficiency, and use an array of teaching methods to help each student discover meaning in lessons.[24] Schools improve when they equip students to assess their own achievement on assignments and when they inspire students to want to learn. Schools improve as a result of establishing alliances with the community and enlisting the help and support of parents.

Traditional public schools belonging to one educational system can deliver an outstanding education. Americans have only to commit to their traditional educational system. If they decide that they want the nation's single system of public schools to achieve high academic and social aims, it will happen.

Modern science offers the general public and educators new ways to think about America's one system of public education. Its discoveries suggest that Americans can, and should, reform existing public schools, not abandon them. Specific recommendations regarding mathematics, science, and foreign languages illustrate ways that traditional public schools can help young people achieve excellence.

NOTES

1. Richard F. Elmore, "Testing Trap," *Harvard Magazine,* September–October 2002: 35.

2. Bonnie and Rebecca, interviewed by Elaine B. Johnson, Summer Contextual Teaching and Learning Conference, University of Alaska, Anchorage, June 2002.

3. Jessica Siegel, "The Community Scholar: Pedro Antonio Noguera Is a 'Pragmatic Optimist' about Urban Schools," *Harvard Magazine*, January–February 2002: 52.

4. William C. Symonds, "Closing the School Gap: If No Child Is to Be Left Behind, We Must Overhaul Funding," *Business Week*, 14 October 2002: 124–25.

5. Symonds, "Closing the School Gap," 124–25.

6. Elmore, "Testing Trap," 37.

7. Lorna Spear, "Improving Bemiss Elementary School," presented at the Washington State School Improvement Conference, Tacoma, 5 November 2002.

8. Spear, "Improving Bemiss Elementary School."

9. Spear, "Improving Bemiss Elementary School."

10. Elmore, "Testing Trap," 33.

11. Spear, "Improving Bemiss Elementary School."

12. Elaine B. Johnson, *Contextual Teaching and Learning: What It Is and Why It's Here to Stay* (Thousand Oaks, Calif.: Corwin Press, Inc., 2002), 26–29.

13. Johnson, *Contextual Teaching and Learning,* 30–32.

14. Johnson, *Contextual Teaching and Learning,* 32–36.

15. Program coordinator, Susan B. Anthony Elementary School, Sacramento, interviewed by Elaine B. Johnson, phone conversation, 18 March 2003. Susan B. Anthony's principal was declared Principal of the Year for the State of California, having been nominated by the Association of California School Administrations.

16. Spear, "Improving Bemiss Elementary School."

17. John E. Chubb and Terry M. Moe, *Politics, Markets, and America's Schools* (Washington, D.C.: Brookings Institution, 1990), 59.

18. David Tyack, cited in Sheila Curran Bernard and Sarah Mondale, *School: The Story of American Public Education,* ed. Sarah Mondale and Sarah B. Patton (Boston: Beacon Press, 2001), 76.

19. Torin M. Finser, *School Renewal: A Spiritual Journey for Change* (Great Barrington, Mass.: Anthroposophic Press, 2001), 103–05.

20. Finser, *School Renewal,* 101–07.

21. Alfie Kohn, *Beyond Discipline: From Compliance to Community* (Alexandria: Association for Supervision and Curriculum Development, 1996), 7.

22. Howard Gardner, *Frames of Mind: The Theory of Multiple Intelligences,* 10th ed. (New York: HarperCollins, 1993), 73–83.

23. Richard Restak, *The Secret Life of the Brain* (New York: Dana Press and Joseph Henry Press, 2002), 71–115.

24. Margaret J. Wheatley, *Leadership and the New Science* (San Francisco: Berrett-Koehler Publishers, 1992), 65, 137.

CHAPTER 5

Good Teaching Connects Lessons with Life: Teaching History, Science, and Foreign Languages in Context

TEACHING THAT HELPS ALL STUDENTS

Most parents seem to have a sense of the kind of education they want for their children, and most parents seem to think that teachers will deliver that education if they choose to do so. Certainly, teachers who work in well-funded traditional public schools, especially schools where everyone is dedicated to the same mission, are in an excellent position to achieve the fundamental aims of quality education—namely, to help all young people master academic subjects and to teach them that human beings are inextricably connected to, and responsible for, one another and the Earth. It is exceedingly difficult, however, for teachers to achieve these educational aims in dilapidated, fragmented public schools. Occasionally, however, even in these circumstances teachers do manage to help students excel.

Parents need to understand what teachers do in their classrooms to help *all* children achieve high academic goals, even in the bleakest conditions. Parents cannot intelligently oversee their child's education unless they are aware of teaching methods that do reach the minds of all young people, including those who learn easily and those who struggle to master academic subjects. This chapter offers parents insights into the remarkable effectiveness of teaching in context—teaching, that is, that connects academic material with students' lives. When teachers galvanize young people into mastering difficult material, as often as not, they do so by teaching in context. Teaching in context—connecting lessons with life—can be done in countless ways. An excellent example of connecting a lesson with life is provided by a public history lecture given at a popular historic site.

LECTURING IN CONTEXT MAKES HISTORY AT THE PARK MEMORABLE

On 22 April 2003, Kirk D. Kehrberg, a park ranger interpreter at Historic Jamestown, located on Jamestown Island, Virginia, delivered a history lecture that captivated a large audience of elementary school students. The adult tourists also delighted in his excellent history lessons. Ranger Kehrberg gathered the audience into a huge semicircle around a landmark, lectured on history, and then led the crowd to the next landmark to lecture again. As he moved from place to place, no one defected, and when he spoke, no one fidgeted or whispered to friends. Adults and children alike were silent and attentive because they wanted to know what the guide would say next. He made history mean something to them.

Ranger Kehrberg helped the children find meaning in Jamestown history by connecting it with the context of their own knowledge and experience. For example, he told his young audience that the smallest of the three ships that brought the original settlers to Jamestown, the *Discovery,* held only twenty-one people:

> How many here have seen a school bus? The ship was about as big as a school bus. The settlers on that small boat bathed only twice a year. Why do you bathe? How often? The settlers thought that bathing too often would harm them. What do you think a school bus would smell like if people lived in it for three months, and no one ever took a bath? Would tempers flare? The Native Americans went swimming in the river twice every day. Who knew best? What kind of an impression do you think the unwashed Europeans made on the Native Americans?

Trying to impress the elementary school children with the severity of martial law in Jamestown, the guide asked, "What's the worst punishment your mother might give you for saying a swear word?" He heard the children's answers and then described his own mother's punishment for swearing. In this way he created a context for explaining that in Jamestown the first punishment for swearing was severe but variable, the second was "to have the tongue pierced through with a bodkin—anyone know what a bodkin is? It's any sharp object such as a knife or nail"—and the third was death. And to suggest possible causes of the enmity that eventually developed between the settlers and the Native Americans, the guide asked, "Have you ever refused to share a candy bar because it was the only one you had and you were really hungry? During a terrible drought, the Native Americans were able to grow only enough corn for themselves, so probably they refused to share their food with the settlers. Can you blame them? Would this have caused the two groups to fight?"[1]

The guide realized that all of the elementary school students he was addressing brought to that Jamestown tour their context of ideas, experiences, and knowledge. He sought to link the children's existing context—their situation—with Jamestown history. Because the children were able to connect facts about the Jamestown settlers with knowledge stored in their long-term memories, the history meant something to them. They cared about it. Chances are good that those children will remember the history lessons the guide presented that day.

The guide's success illustrates the power of teaching and learning in context. Teaching in context is nothing new, of course. Good teachers invariably place academic material in the context of their students' personal, social, and cultural circumstances. Only recently, however, has science clarified the enormous importance of context in virtually everything we do. Before the twentieth century, as physicist Lee Smolin explains, human beings did not know "that the stars are organized into galaxies, . . . that the continents move, or that genetic information is stored in DNA, and they had only the faintest notions of the history of life on Earth." Human beings did not know that "gravity could be merely an aspect of how space and time are arranged, . . . [or know] how atoms or stars worked, and they had heard of neither the quantum nor the atomic nucleus."[2]

There is far more to Earth and the cosmos than was dreamed of in philosophies based on classical nineteenth-century physics and biology. Today new science indicates that each of the three principles active throughout the universe and Earth—the principles of interrelatedness, self-organization, and differentiation—points to the importance of context. After defining *context,* I consider the rich implications of these three principles for classroom instruction.[3]

MODERN SCIENCE EXPLAINS CONTEXT

Context derives from the Latin *contexere,* meaning "to weave together." The word *context,* then, indicates that everything is related to everything else. The actions, words, objects, and individuals in a particular space at a particular time are woven together. When we are open and receptive to the many different contexts we inhabit, those of family, friends, clubs, teams, neighborhoods, and the workplace, each context has the capacity to change our point of view. Being receptive to context requires noticing the attitude we bring to an event or experience, looking for meaning while we are engaged, and later reflecting on the significance of the context.

Our response to any event, place, or experience—any context— reflects, of course, our Self: our personality, unconscious assumptions, emotional makeup, beliefs, and view of the world. Teaching methods that speak to each student's unique self, that connect academic material with a student's interests, knowledge, and experience, generate academic success. Teaching in context is a pathway to academic excellence that all young people can follow. Modern science tells us why context is so important to teaching and learning.[4]

Interrelatedness and Context

The principle of interrelatedness recognized by twentieth-century scientists affirms that all things exist in relation to one another. They exist, that is, in context. This context, this web of relationships, gives things their meaning. The meaning a person has when he or she is in the context of family differs from the meaning he or she has as part of a team on the assembly line at Toyota or as third baseman on the neighborhood softball team. "It is the context," as biologist Gregory Bateson has written, "that fixes the meaning."[5]

The context human beings inhabit completes the Self. Context affects how people regard themselves, interact with others, and view the world. It shapes their intellectual abilities, personality traits, and emotional makeup. It imprints their values and attitudes. The Chilean biologist Humberto Maturana cautions us to take seriously the impact of environment on Self. Moment by moment a child's Self arises, he explains, in response to the relationships that form that child's context: "We adults create history, our children carry it. We create the present that the children experience, and then they make history. They will make whatever world they will make according to how they have lived their childhood. . . . How we are with our children alters . . . how human history goes."[6]

Because context influences our values and perspectives, we must make a conscious effort to assess the point of view that guides us. Do facts support this point of view? Does convincing evidence lend weight to it? Does new knowledge require that we look at things from a changed perspective? In addition to asking what picture of the world shall guide us through each day, we must recognize our capacity to design and alter context. Our support for, or objections to, America's recent invasion of Iraq can affect the country's context as surely as a teacher's gentle voice can shape the context of a classroom.

Teachers who understand that everything is interrelated, forming various contexts, see their students differently, and teach differently, than do those who are oblivious to the interrelatedness of existence. They realize that mutual respect, collaboration, and inquiry are natural to young children and encourage such behavior.

Self-Organization and Context

Like the principle of interrelatedness, the principle of self-organization also suggests ways that teachers, emulating nature's processes, can take advantage of context to help students see meaning in their lessons. Self-organization is the capacity of living systems, including human beings, to adjust and react to their context—their immediate environment—in ways that enable them not only to survive, maintaining their essential uniqueness, but also to develop their potential. If a living creature is free, then it can self-organize. If it is tightly constrained by external forces, then it cannot. Teachers familiar with the principle of self-organization know that children who have opportunities to make choices, explore ideas, test hypotheses, ask good questions, and think carefully about details are able to develop their full potential as they acquire the knowledge that raises IQ. Such teachers give children many chances to connect lessons with the context of daily life.

Connecting lessons with their own lives helps young people learn to adjust their thinking as they gain new information. As self-organizing systems, human beings need to be free to analyze and weigh what they learn and to change their point of view in response to new information. Human beings continuously self-organize as they react to their immediate context. They adapt, change, alter their beliefs, and explore their potential, all the while retaining their fundamental identity. Teachers who understand that human beings are self-organizing see how natural it is to teach students to link academic subjects with their own circumstances. They make it a point to know about these circumstances by paying close attention to their students at school and away from school. Obviously, the more insight teachers have into a student's personal situation, the better the connections they can make between academic subjects and that student's life.

Differentiation and Context

The principle of differentiation describes the universe's lavishly creative drive toward ever-increasing newness and complexity. This principle is evident in the unexpected structures that have emerged from a teeming Earth. It is evident in the diversity that we admire when we walk among wildflowers, hear a new musical composition, or sit in a crowded football stadium. The principle of differentiation impels us to create. It urges us to make our own contribution to the world's fabulous diversity.

Teachers who are aware of the principle of differentiation realize that diversity is a fundamental sign of life's richness and health and a major source of their school's exuberance and creativity. They recognize that a rich educational context consists of young people from a wide range of different cultures, races, and social circumstances. These diverse students gain from one another insights and meanings they would surely have missed had they not come to know and appreciate one another. A diverse context, characterized by vitality and excitement, has the power to ignite the creative promise residing in every human being.

Good teachers keep their eye on context. They pay attention to the interrelatedness that enables human beings to find meaning in context, to the self-organization that makes it possible for potential to emerge in context, and to the differentiation that enriches context, inspiring creativity. Paying attention to context makes it possible for teachers to give every child a quality education.

THE ELEMENTS OF CONTEXTUAL TEACHING

Teaching that concentrates on the context of students' daily lives involves more, however, than creating meaning for students by linking new academic material with existing information. Teaching in context involves helping students enlarge their experience by using schoolwork to achieve significant purposes. Contextual teaching occurs both in traditional classroom sessions and in active, self-regulated learning activities. Self-regulated learners lead, organize, investigate, and make decisions. They look to their teachers not for answers, but for advice and encouragement. To become active learners, students must know how to work together as well as alone, and they must practice thinking critically and systematically rather than act on assumptions. Contextual teaching and learning asks students to recognize and meet high standards, and it invites them to demonstrate their knowledge and skills by offering presentations and performances to specific audiences.

Teaching in context requires above all that teachers know their students. Teachers must know each student's situation at school and at home, as well as the student's specific experiences, skills, and tastes. Knowing students well makes it possible for teachers to appeal to their individual interests, talents, and learning styles.

IS THERE AN EASY WAY TO LEARN HARD SUBJECTS?

Virtually everyone today—parents, educators, business leaders, and policy makers—believes that all young people, not just the intellectually gifted, are entitled to and urgently need to master such demanding academic subjects as science, foreign languages, and mathematics. Only a sound grasp of science, foreign languages, and mathematics will equip young people to make ethical, intelligent decisions in a diverse, turbulent world being molded constantly by new science and changing technology.

Since the early 1980s, research and experience have shown that contextual teaching and learning is a remarkably effective way to help all students reach high academic standards.[7] For example, Dr. Todd Duncan, who teaches cosmology and physics at Portland State University in Oregon, Dr. David Gurney, a professor who trains foreign language teachers in the College of Education at the University of Central Florida, and Mrs. Judith Reihard, an award-winning mathematics teacher in Tempe, Arizona, agree that teaching in context is the surest way to make difficult academic material accessible to *all* students. They have found that when students are given a chance to learn science, foreign languages, and mathematics by connecting academic content to the context of their immediate situations, the probability is high that students will master these subjects. This chapter discusses teaching science and foreign languages in context. Chapter 6 offers concrete suggestions for making mathematics accessible to all students from kindergarten through university.

Everybody Learns Science in Context

According to Dr. Duncan, all students in the twenty-first century, not just the intellectually elite, must understand key scientific principles and be capable of applying them to events and decisions they will encounter as adults.[8] One way students learn science and how to apply it to their own lives involves becoming aware of what they already know about a topic before the teacher tackles it in class. Preliminary questions such as "What do you know or think about this subject already?" and "How do you think this works?" make students conscious of the context, the web of ideas and assumptions, they bring to the study of science. These questions help students notice that as they learn science, their point of view alters—and with it their interpretation of the world. An introductory question for children learning about the seasons on Earth, for example, might be, "What do you think causes the seasons?"

An astronomy professor might preface instruction with an assignment asking students first to imagine that they are floating away from the Earth and have an unobstructed view of all of space and then to answer the questions, "What objects do you see? What size, color, and arrangement do these objects have?" These questions invite students to draw on information they have picked up from such sources as movies, television programs, books, other classes, and conversations. The questions ask students to speculate in ways that create a frame of reference, or context, for the answers that science provides.

Another strategy that helps students learn science is to ask them to solve real problems that scientists have actually faced and conquered. From working on these problems, because it broadens their experience, students find meaning in what had been remote abstract concepts. An example of putting a scientific problem in a student's immediate context is provided by one of the greatest triumphs of the science of astronomy. This triumph is astronomy's ability to measure some of the vast distances to the planets, stars, and galaxies visible in the night sky. Students are best able to comprehend what these distances really mean and to appreciate the techniques for measuring them if their first assignment is to look at the stars and invent their own method for measuring the distance to the brightest star they see. Trying to solve this real problem gives students firsthand experience of the difficulties scientists encountered when they tried to determine the distance to a point of light without being able to draw on a sense of scale.

In physics class, the study of the laws of motion entails manipulating concepts of position and time that typically strike students as dry, abstract, and remote from their world. Asking groups of students to invent their own clocks by using everyday materials and by drawing on some common features of nature helps them assign concrete significance to an abstraction. Students working in groups have invented many remarkable clocks. One clock, for instance, consisted of a weight hanging from a string. The swings of the weight marked the passage of time. Another clock required measuring time by keeping track of the changes in the height of a burning candle. For every invention, students made up units of time based on their unique clock. This experiment enabled students to attach concrete meaning to the parameter t for time that shows up in equations describing the laws of motion. Consequently, the parameter t seemed more clearly a part of their world. The experiment also taught students that our present system for measuring time was designed by people who chose processes in nature that record the passage of time and standardized them to develop our familiar unit of seconds and minutes.

Using schoolwork to address community problems also gives students a context that assigns meaning to science, thus making it intelligible. When the city of Portland, Oregon, for example, was considering changes in its transportation system to reduce air pollution, it asked Portland State University students for their advice. To produce sound recommendations, students learned science and then applied their scientific concepts in concrete situations for practical reasons. Connecting academic lessons to a significant community problem gave them a real context that made abstract science concepts accessible to every student.

Because learning in context makes science intelligible to everyone, science is no longer the exclusive domain of those who delight in abstractions. By studying science in context, all students see concrete evidence that the world that science investigates is the same world that they inhabit. Distance—whether calculated to the moon by trigonometry or covered by walking—is the same concept. The photons scientists describe in physics are the same photons we experience every time we look at something. Ultimately, every valuable result derived from science can be linked to our individual, direct experience. Science classes that involve learning in context help all students become aware of these links. They instill in all students an awareness that science will inevitably shape the worldview that bears on everything they see and do.

Everybody Learns Foreign Languages in Context

Those who do not understand basic science are severely limited by their inability to make informed judgments about cloning, genetic research, environmental policies, or any of the other scientific and technical issues that people read about in the news every day. In the same way, those who do not know foreign languages are severely limited. They are limited by their inability to understand and communicate with people belonging to cultures that differ from their own. In a nation of great diversity and in a world of myriad cultures and races, it is incumbent on every person to understand as many cultures as possible. Foreign language teachers are acutely mindful, of course, that knowing a second language nurtures such understanding. They recognize, furthermore, that communicating in a new language entails the ability not only to read and write the language but also to speak it fluently.[9]

Their search for the best way to teach young people to speak a new language has led many instructors to agree that speaking a language for a reason that holds meaning in the present moment—using language in context—helps all students gain proficiency. Professor David Gurney, an expert on teaching language in context, says that students learn best when "every use of language is tied to some naturally occurring purpose."[10] When students engage in naturally occurring, purposeful conversation that bears on the context of their daily lives, they diligently acquire new language patterns and words. Wishing to interact with others in significant ways, they have a concrete, practical reason to acquire new language forms.

Learning language by focusing on things that hold meaning for students—acquiring words in order to convey personal beliefs, describe events, and express feelings—seems to be much more effective than the rote memorization of lists of words out of context is. Students who interact with one another and the teacher for a significant purpose are motivated to become skilled interpreters and speakers of a new language. Young children, for example, easily learn days of the week when they are asked to describe the things they do on particular days. Given a chance to make statements that are about their own lives, children naturally want to learn grammar and vocabulary so that they can express their meaning clearly.[11] Students learn a new language not only when it bears directly on their present world but also when they expand their world by studying the culture of the language they are learning. Culture manifests itself, of course, in architecture, pictures, songs, literature, symbols, values, ceremonies, music, and humor. It is evident in ideas of tragedy, beauty, love, and spirit. Because language and culture are inseparable, studying culture necessarily gives rise to language. Familiarity with the culture underlying a language provides a meaningful context for speaking that language.

Of course, it is possible to learn about an unfamiliar culture in many ways. For example, a group of high school students might search the

World Wide Web to locate French newspaper editorials and articles dealing with some current issue that also concerns the United States. A group of students might then present the French point of view and lead class discussion on this subject. Similarly, if young students know they will be dining with classmates and their teacher at a local Mexican restaurant where only Spanish is spoken, then they have a real incentive to learn useful vocabulary words and grammatical constructions. Using a new language for a real purpose helps students see meaning in their study and encourages them to become fluent.

Although many Americans have for decades held the insular view that they do not need to learn a foreign language, today we recognize that learning new languages is essential to living harmoniously in a pluralistic American society and to living among other nations in a small global society. Gone are the days when only students thought to have a special aptitude for languages were encouraged to speak them. Today traditional public schools have an obligation to see that all students become proficient not only in English but also in at least one other language. Furthermore, children for whom English is a second language must be guaranteed opportunities to increase proficiency both in English and in their first language.[12] If all American students learn at least one new language, then their ability to appreciate other races and cultures will increase markedly. As their appreciation and understanding grow, so will their ability to maintain America's democracy and to respect members of various nations and cultures.

EVERYONE CAN EXCEL

For some reason, students often conclude, even before they reach high school, that they are not the stuff of which scientists, linguists, and mathematicians are made. Convinced of their intellectual limitations, they resign themselves to ignorance and give up, effectively slamming the door on countless vocations and avocations. Perhaps educators and parents might benefit from remembering that a normal child's brain is by definition intelligent. It has, after all, achieved the astonishing feat of acquiring a native language. How could it not be intelligent? The intelligent human brain is genetically disposed to learn. It learns every time it attaches meaning to new events and information. Meaning is not intrinsic in history, or science, or languages. Humans assign meaning to these things. They assign meaning to a subject when they link it with the context of their own lives today. Once young people see meaning in their studies, they are able to perform well on even the most difficult assignments.

This chapter explores the power of teaching and learning in context by looking at strategies designed to help *every* student find meaning in the study of science and foreign languages. Connecting science and foreign languages to students' lives in the immediate moment motivates young people to do their best in school. Given a reason to learn academic material, students are inspired to excel.

Chapter 6 offers further evidence of the effectiveness of connecting schoolwork with real life. It provides examples of practical strategies that mathematics teachers use to give meaning to their subject and thus to transform anxious mathematics students into confident mathematicians. Chapter 6 also points out that mastery of mathematics, science, foreign languages, or any other academic subject requires both deep understanding and the ability to think critically. The ability to think critically, a skill neglected in many schools, is an important attribute of the truly educated person.

NOTES

1. I have paraphrased here the remarks of Interpretive Park Ranger Kirk D. Kehrberg, Jamestown Historic Park on Jamestown Island, a part of Colonial National Historical Park in Virginia. Kehrberg made these remarks during his presentation on 22 April 2003. His use of context helps him bring history to life.

2. Lee Smolin, *The Life of the Cosmos* (New York: Widenfeld and Nicolson, 1997), 157.

3. For more information about new science, see Michael Colebrook, "The New Universe Story," available at www.greenspirit.org.uk (accessed 3 April 2003).

4. Elaine B. Johnson, *Contextual Teaching and Learning: What It Is and Why It's Here to Stay* (Thousand Oaks, Calif.: Corwin Press, Inc., 2002), 11–46.

5. Gregory Bateson, *Mind and Nature: A Necessary Unity* (New York: Bantam Books, 1990), 17.

6. Humberto Maturana and Pille Bunnell, "Biosphere, Homosphere, and Robosphere: What Has That to Do with Business?" available at www.sol-ne.org/res/wp/maturana (accessed January 1999), 1–28 (based on a presentation made by Humberto Maturana to the Society for Organizational Learning Members' Meeting, Amherst, Mass., June 1998).

7. For a history of contextual teaching and its elements, see Johnson, *Contextual Teaching and Learning,* 1–13, 23–25.

8. This discussion of science relies on Todd Duncan, "Contextual Teaching and Learning of Science," unpublished MS, 2003, 1–11. Duncan holds a Ph.D. in astrophysics from the University of Chicago. He created these assignments for university and high school students. He is the author of *An Ordinary World: The Role of Science in Your Search for Personal Meaning* and coauthor with a colleague at the University of Chicago of an as-yet-unpublished astronomy textbook for college students that is now being piloted at two universities. Duncan is president of the Science Integration Institute in Hillsboro, Oreg. (www.scienceintegration.org). For additional information on teaching science in context, see, for example, American Association for the Advancement of Science, *The Liberal Art of Science: Agenda for Action* (Washington, D.C.: American Association for the Advancement of Science, 1990); National Research Council, *National Science Education Standards* (Washington, D.C.: National Academy Press, 1996); M. Suzanne Donovan, John D. Bransford, and James Peggegrino, eds., *How People Learn: Bridging Research and Practice* (Washington, D.C.: National Academy Press, 1999); and Art Hobson, *Physics: Concepts and Connections* (Englewood Cliffs, N.J.: Prentice-Hall, 1998).

9. The national standards for foreign language education have influenced instructional activities aimed at oral communication. To appreciate these national standards and their effect on foreign language instruction, see, for example, American Council on the Teaching of Foreign Languages, *National Standards for Foreign Language Education* (New York: American Council on the Teaching of Foreign Languages, 1999); and June K. Phillips and Robert M. Terry, eds., *Foreign Language Standards: Linking Research, Theories, and Practices* (Lincolnwood, Ill.: National Textbook Co. and American Council on the Teaching of Foreign Languages, 1999). For insights into the contextual teaching of languages, see, for example, David W. Gurney, "Total Immersion of Welcome Outsiders: Cross-Cultural Encounters," in *A TESOL Professional Anthology,* ed. Carol Cargill (Lincolnwood, Ill.: Volunitad Publishers and National Textbook Co., 1987), 113–20; Wilga Rivers, *A Practical Guide to the Teaching of French* (Lincolnwood, Ill.: National Textbook Co.,

1968); Claire Kramsch, "Second Language Acquisition, Applied Linguistics, and the Teaching of Foreign Languages," *Modern Language Journal* 84, no. 3 (September 2000): 310–15; and Alice Omaggio-Handley, *Teaching Language in Context* (Boston: Heinle and Heinle, 1986).

10. David W. Gurney, "Culture as the Context for Teaching Foreign Languages," unpublished MS, 2003, 15. For material on teaching foreign languages, I have made extensive use of this work. In this paper Gurney provides many examples of teaching language in context and also an extensive analysis of competing theories about the teaching of languages, a concern given impetus by the appearance of the national standards for foreign languages in 1999.

11. Gurney, "Culture as the Context for Teaching Foreign Languages," 18, 27.

12. Gurney, "Culture as the Context for Teaching Foreign Languages," 1.

CHAPTER 6

Mathematics and Clear Thinking for Everyone

DEFINING AN EDUCATED PERSON

Everybody wants America's children to receive a quality education. The problem is that the general public cannot agree about what a truly educated person looks like. Many journalists, policy makers, and business leaders equate education with earning a high score on a statewide standardized achievement test. Performing well on these tests certainly takes a sharp memory and quick recall. That is why more and more teachers constantly drill students to retain information and why they routinely use class time to give practice tests. The attention teachers give to memorizing and practicing takes up so much time that little remains for creative teaching. Teachers know that regurgitating isolated facts, recognizing vocabulary words, and following steps to solve problems are exercises that require slight, if any, understanding of a subject. They know, too, that in their professional world of rewards and punishments for student performance on test scores, creative teaching is not expedient. It is risky to spend class time giving students opportunities to inquire, search for solutions, and connect school assignments to their personal beliefs and interests. Safety resides in being satisfied with drilling students to memorize, for instance, new vocabulary words for a multiple-choice achievement test. Students can perform well on such a test without understanding how to use the new vocabulary words in essays or speeches. Unless an educational system requires students to understand the subjects they study and to think well about them, its students will not become truly educated. Fortunately, the mathematics community recognizes that memorizing steps to solve problems is not an end in itself. Under-standing the concepts behind the steps is the goal.

HELPING EVERYONE LEARN MATHEMATICS

The mathematics community, when it formulated its national stan-dards, gave a good deal of attention to pedagogy. Work on pedagogy continues to have a positive influence on teaching, even in the face of pressure on teachers to speed through facts in fat textbooks. Regarding it as a means to help everybody learn mathematics, the mathematics community advises teaching in context. Connecting abstract mathe-matical ideas with the context of students' daily lives, it is suggested, helps students see meaning in, and thus comprehend, mathematics. Whether students handle manipulatives, design projects for competi-tion, create products to benefit the community, or connect mathematics with subjects they study in other classes, when they actively apply mathematical concepts to real situations, they gain a firm understand-ing of these concepts.[1] Because mathematics, perhaps more than sci-ence or foreign languages, seems to intimidate students, this chapter provides several examples of how to teach mathematics in context to students from elementary school through university.

STRATEGIES FOR CONNECTING MATHEMATICS TO STUDENTS' LIVES

Using Manipulatives

Perhaps the most widely used form of active learning to make math-ematics tangible and familiar is the use of manipulatives. For years el-ementary school teachers have used manipulatives—any objects one can touch, move, stack, count, or otherwise handle—primarily to teach children to count and sort. Manipulatives are also a valuable means of teaching young children about data analysis and graphs. To put data analysis and graphs in a context familiar to children, using small pack-ages of candy helps. Children seem especially to enjoy working with a candy called 'Dem Bones, marketed during the Halloween season.

Give the children their own packages of 'Dem Bones. Each package of 'Dem Bones contains five different parts of a skeleton: skull, hand, foot, leg bone, and rib cage. Ask the children to sort the parts of the skeleton and show them how to record the parts on the table shown in figure 6.1. As they record the parts, children create a bar graph that represents the number of each type of candy in their package. It is important to ask questions that encourage the children to think about the relationships they discover: "Which kind of candy do you have more of in your package? How can you tell that from your graph? Do you have an equal number of any two candies?" When children compare their own graphs with those of other students, they discover that not every package of candy is exactly the same.

Noting facts about their own package of candy holds meaning for children because they can connect the facts with their own immediate experience. Placing graphing lessons in the context of their personal tastes in food also adds meaning to schoolwork. To graph

Figure 6.1. 'Dem Bones Table

children's tastes, hang a large graph on the wall, putting it within the children's reach. The chart should contain each child's name and four different flavors of pudding. Each child tastes all four flavors and then places an X on the chart indicating his or her favorite flavor. In this way the children create a graph of data about themselves. Because the graph is about them, about their own preferences, they remember its lessons.

In the later primary grades, learning fractions and how to manipulate them is a difficult hurdle for many students. However, when teachers help students discover that abstract fractions are part of their familiar world, children surmount this hurdle. Students quickly learn, for instance, the *need* to find a common denominator when adding two denominators, and they seem quickly to master the *skills* involved in finding that common denominator, when they work with a 1.55 oz. Hershey's milk chocolate bar.[2] Give each child a candy bar. Ask the children to count the number of rectangular pieces in their own bar. As the candy bar in figure 6.2 shows, the bar contains twelve pieces. Ask the children what part of the whole each of those pieces represents. The answer is one-twelfth (1/12). Ask the children to work in pairs. One child breaks a candy bar in fourths, and the other breaks a candy bar in thirds. A probable way that might happen is shown in the top part of figure 6.3. The two children take one of the fourths (1/4) from one candy bar and one of the thirds (1/3) from the other bar and put them together, as shown at the bottom of figure 6.3.

The children are now ready to figure out what part of the original candy bar they have. If each of the pieces is one-twelfth of the whole

Figure 6.2. *Twelve-Piece Bar. Chocolate bar design is a trademark used with permission of Hershey Foods Corporation.*

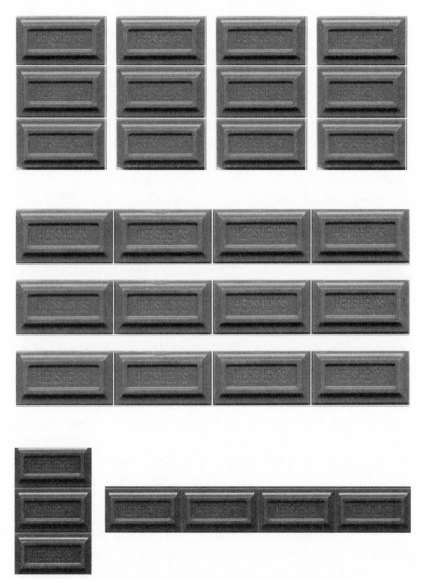

Figure 6.3. Fourths and Thirds, Apart and Combined. Chocolate bar design is a trademark used with permission of Hershey Foods Corporation.

candy bar, then how many of those original small pieces do they have? The answer is "seven of the original twelve pieces" or seven-twelfths (7/12) of the candy bar. This physical process of finding a common denominator when adding fractions helps children see relationships and meaning in their study of fractions. They have tangible evidence that one-fourth of the candy bar is the same as three-twelfths and that one-third of the candy bar is the same as four-twelfths. Having made this discovery, the children are ready to create their own algorithm for changing a fraction to a new denominator. When they develop an algorithm based on their understanding of fractions, the concept becomes theirs. The algorithm means something to them.

Just as the use of manipulatives helps elementary school children understand fractions by connecting them to their own experience, so manipulatives help children actively construct a context that helps them understand a standard measure ruler. For this exercise, each student needs an 8½″ × 11″ sheet of paper. Begin by asking the children to fold their paper in half, matching the short sides. Ask the children how many parts they have divided the paper into and what fraction is represented by the crease. Open the paper and place that fraction on the crease. Fold the paper in half again and then fold it once more. Now the paper is divided into four parts, and the creases are represented by the fractions 1/4, 2/4, and 3/4. Fold the paper as it was—in four parts—and then fold it once again. The paper is now divided into eight parts, and the creases are represented by the fractions 1/8, 2/8, 3/8, 4/8, 5/8, 6/8, and 7/8. Fold the paper once again to produce fractions that are consecutive sixteenths. When students compare a standard ruler with the results from the folding activity, as is shown in figure 6.4, they see that the longest line of fractions is at the half-inch mark on the manipulative and that the longest vertical bar on the ruler represents one-half. Just as the next longest lines of fractions are for the fourths, so the next longest vertical bars on the ruler also represent the fourths. Point out to students that on the manipulative, furthermore, the fractions at the top of each column of fractions are the ones that are used. The numerators of these fractions are always odd numbers, while the denominators of these fractions are even numbers.

Any activity that gives tangible meaning to an abstract mathematical concept is valuable not only for elementary and middle school stu-

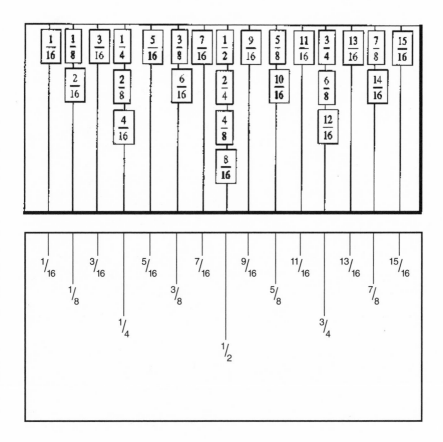

Figure 6.4. *Results of Paper Folding and Standard Ruler*

dents but also for high school and university students. In his university physics class, for example, a professor brought the concept of the trigonometric sine curve to life when he connected a gas supply to a hollow twelve-foot pipe in which quarter-inch holes had been drilled approximately two inches apart. He turned on the gas supply and put a match to one of the holes, causing a four-inch flame to appear at each of the holes. When he hit the pipe with a hammer, the flames immediately appeared as the sine curve. By giving the sine curve visual reality, the professor helped his students understand and retain the concept.

Physical Movement and Abstract Ideas

Another visual means of conveying an abstract concept involves asking students to play a part in representing a mathematical idea. Many second-year algebra teachers place students in particular locations to teach such areas of graphing as linear functions, linear inequalities, absolute value functions, conics, transformations, sine and cosine curves, and derivatives. The teacher uses a large expanse to lay out a coordinate axis. Rather than use dots made by pencil or pen, the teacher asks students to stand in certain positions to represent data points.

A popular way to give mathematics concrete meaning involves moving students around in ways that teach the significance of an ellipse. An ellipse is defined as the set of all points such that the sum of the distances from the foci is constant. An example is shown in figure 6.5. The teacher gives two students a rope that represents the sum of the lengths of the distances from the foci. They hold the rope, one at each end, and stand at two points that represent the foci (A and B). The third student (point C) takes the rope, keeping it tight between him- or herself and the other two students, and walks around the other two students in the elliptical path that the rope allows. Student C places corn or beans on the floor following the path as he or she walks. The path and the dropped corn are in the shape of an ellipse. As the students gain understanding of the concept, they are asked to change their positions or the length of the rope to determine how the shape of the curve changes given different parameters. Encouraging students to create an ellipse with their bodies connects the mathematical concept to movement. The idea becomes a kind of sensation.

Using Mathematics to Produce Significant Products

Many teachers provide high school students with a significant purpose for learning mathematics. For example, a calculus teacher motivated his students to learn calculus by asking them to work in groups to produce designs for a trash dumpster that the school would commission to be made. The winning design had to provide the greatest volume for the least cost.

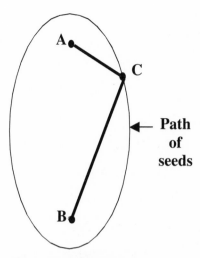

Figure 6.5. *An Elliptical Path*

To help students learn algebra, geometry, and trigonometry, many teachers in Arizona supervised teams of students from their respective high schools in a competition to build solar-powered boats. Eleven competing teams worked with the same basic specifications. They were judged, among other things, for their boat's performance and style, the technical writing they generated, and their oral presentation explaining how they designed their boat. Clearly, if the students' application of mathematics faltered, then their whole project would be compromised.[3]

Further evidence that students learn mathematics when they are actively engaged in work that holds meaning for them is provided by geography students at McClintock High School in Tempe, Arizona. Since 1987 geography students have been painting U.S. and world maps on playground cement pads at primary and middle schools throughout the Phoenix metropolitan area (see figure 6.6). These maps are drawn to scale and are painted in patterns using from four to seven different colors. The area available on which the map can be painted determines the scale to be used for the map. Students mark off a grid using a chalk line and then paint the map portions according to their predetermined color pattern; they use a type of paint that actually stains the cement. The measurements of the maps are usually close to 88' x 94'.

Figure 6.6. *Outdoor Map by McClintock High School Students*

Although the obvious point of this exercise is to give high school students an immediate, significant reason to learn geography, it has the added benefit of teaching them mathematics and of having them discover the satisfaction of benefiting others. The elementary and middle schools value these maps and put them to use in many ways. For instance, they use them in games such as "Where Are You (or Your Parents) From?" or "Name That State." Some schools have added landforms such as mountains, deserts, and rivers to their maps. "Bike across the United States," a project that has students riding their bicycles around the school track, gives students a better understanding of geography, distances, and location. The children mark two cities on the map, calculate the distance between them, and, in relays, ride that distance on their school track. To date, McClintock students have painted sixty-three maps for schools in their region.[4]

Looking at Mathematics in Your Favorite Subject

One reason that *all* children, those who enjoy mathematics and those who struggle to learn it, must become adept mathematicians is that mathematics is ubiquitous, as surely as words are ubiquitous. The literature, visual arts, and music that so many math-shy students do enjoy hold even more richness for them when they know mathematics. Educators increasingly realize the effectiveness of teaching mathematics in the context of these subjects. Doing so makes it possible for students to find meaning in mathematics by connecting it to disciplines that speak to them.

To promote the interdisciplinary study of mathematics, Dartmouth College obtained funding from the National Science Foundation. From 1995 to 2002, Dartmouth faculty integrated mathematics into a wide array of courses ranging from music and architecture to earth sciences and English. Students could choose from among such classes as "Mathematics and Science Fiction: The Fire in the Equations," "How Many Angels? Mathematics, Philosophy and the Infinite," the Spanish literature course "A Matter of Time," and a studio art class that involved examining the math involved in various design patterns.[5] Placing mathematics in the context of literature, the visual arts, and music helps everyone—from very young children to adults—take it to heart.

Literature

Many novels written for children and young adults lend themselves to teaching mathematical concepts and techniques. Margaret Wise Brown's classic *The Runaway Bunny,* for example, exposes preschoolers to mathematical logic because it is written in a format that uses *if-then* statements: *If you are a blitz, then you are a curd. If you are a curd, then you are a merf. If you are a merf, then you are a plet. Conclusion: If you are a blitz, then you are a plet.* Children are quick to appreciate nonsense, of course, and easily follow the process of reaching a conclusion from a group of *if-then* claims. As they follow the *if-then* sequence, they are learning a mathematical process that plays a crucial role in the study of logic, as figure 6.7 shows.

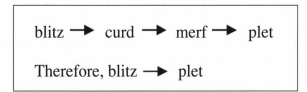

Figure 6.7. *If-Then Conclusions*

The underlying premise of Natalie Babbitt's popular fantasy *Tuck Everlasting* invites students to think about mathematical concepts. In this fantasy, the Tuck family is able to live forever without changing. Their situation raises for young people a number of questions that carry mathematical significance:

> What would happen if all of this generation's children lived forever? Would additional children be born? Would the world population change over the next 100 years? What is the ideal age? Would the world cultures and populations change? How many years is a generation? Has the length of a generation changed over the years? And what is meant by a generation gap? What are the stages in our lives? Have the lengths of those stages changed? What is the total expected life span?

As students learn mathematics to deal with some of these questions, they also discover their own beliefs about society.

The enduring science fiction novel *Flatland: A Romance of Many Dimensions,* which appeared first in 1884, also gives meaning to mathematics by linking it with students' interests. The characters in this book are geometric figures whose exploits draw readers into learning mathematical concepts and their relationships. The protagonist is A. Square, a two dimensional figure, who discovers the existence of the third dimension and is encouraged to think of a fourth dimension.

Music Is Math

Students of all ages who study music with the intent of becoming virtuoso performers or of composing their own music have a special incentive to learn mathematics. Mathematics is integral to music. Music notes obey the boundaries of a measure, and that measure is divided by using notes of varying value: quarter notes, eighth notes, sixteenths, and so on. The very process of transposing music into a different key can be related to transformational geometry. Figure 6.8 shows the first few measures of "Twinkle, Twinkle, Little Star," written in the key of C, and a numeric graph of the notes, where middle C is at zero. When the music is transposed to the key of F and the two versions of the music are graphed together (figure 6.9), one is able to see that the key of F is a translation, better known as a slide, of the key of C.

Figure 6.8. *Numeric Graph of "Twinkle, Twinkle, Little Star" in the Key of C*

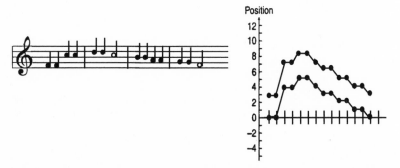

Figure 6.9. *Numeric Graphs of "Twinkle, Twinkle, Little Star" in the Keys of C and F*

When two notes have frequencies in a ratio of 2:1, they are said to have perfect harmony. The second most harmonic ratio is that of 3:2. The existence of a melody in a song and the note repetitions required to repeat that melody are very similar to geometric translations. Furthermore, the very idea of creating music from a vast selection of note arrangements lends itself to the inclusion of combinatorics in the study of music. All of these ideas give meaning to mathematics for those taking music classes.

Art and Mathematics

The process of creating a two-dimensional drawing of a three-dimensional object is related to mathematics. The principles of composition and design involved in the process of organizing a pictorial space afford opportunities to teach mathematical concepts. Indeed, typically, mathematics textbooks contain in their chapters on ratio and proportion a discussion of these in Michelangelo's paintings and sculpture. Just as painters use ratios and proportions in their compositions, so they use ratios and proportions to gauge the chemical composition of their materials.

These examples suggest that America's traditional public school system does well to support and encourage teachers who connect subjects such as mathematics, science, and foreign languages to the context of students' lives. Such teachers help *all* children master rigorous academic material. At the same time, they teach young people to think well, the sign of a truly educated person.

THINKING WELL ABOUT THINKING

When students learn mathematics in context, they do so thoughtfully. They question, speculate, experiment, reason logically, deliberate, interpret, explain, compare, and solve problems. They think long and hard. The same is true when they study science, foreign languages, literature, or any other discipline with the intention of fully understanding it. Thinking is what human beings do. Some humans, however, think more precisely, clearly, systematically, and objectively than others do. The more skilled one is at thinking, the more hopeful one's own circumstances are. Thinking well makes it possible for people to get through each day making wise, informed decisions. During these early years of the twenty-first century, America could use some good thinkers to make wise decisions.

The Urgent Need for Clear Thinking

How will young people become confident adults living capable, purposeful lives if America's single system of public education fails to teach them to think systematically, honestly, and objectively? Alarming numbers of this nation's children live in fractured homes. Unable to turn to an adult for advice, they rely on the advice of their peers and the values of television. It is common knowledge, certainly, that television programs and commercials discourage logical thought, distort reality, and make children insensitive to ugly images that twenty years ago would have caused revulsion. Many television programs teach young people that violence is an inevitable, routine part of ordinary life. According to a 1992 study published in the *Journal of the American Medical Association,* "The introduction of television in the 1950s caused a subsequent doubling of the homicide rate."[6] Its calculation notes that it took fifteen years for violent television images to transform a two-year-old child into a seventeen-year-old murderer.

One of the best defenses young people can have against the miseducation of television is the ability to think well, a facility encouraged, among other things, by independent learning activities that place academic subjects in the context of real life. David Perkins, recipient of a grant from the MacArthur Foundation, notes that "trivial pursuit makes a metaphor for many features of contemporary education."[7] Perkins reminds educators that, instead of covering many facts, "learning is a consequence of thinking" and only thinking will produce educated citizens. Lawrence A. Cremin urges educators to teach young people critical thinking when he warns that "modern culture . . . [has] thrown men and women into a 'collective dream' from which they [can] . . . escape only by prodigious exercise of critical intelligence."[8] Educators must give young people not only a store of facts but also the critical intelligence to use them in various contexts.

Critical intelligence encompasses the ability to develop hypotheses, question assumptions, recognize convincing evidence, analyze the logic of an argument, identify biases, and consider the implications of conclusions. It includes knowing how to speculate, question, interpret, infer, and synthesize information. Critical thinking makes it possible to transfer knowledge from one situation to a different, unfamiliar context. Critical thinkers "view a situation from several perspectives, . . . attend to the context in which . . . [they] are perceiving information, and eventually . . . create new categories through which this information may be understood."[9] When students have opportunities to connect academic disciplines with the context of their own lives, they "make the material meaningful to themselves."[10]

Parents must *demand* that public schools teach their children to think critically. They must insist that schools give their children not only the factual information that standardized tests try to measure but also the critical intelligence that makes it possible for human beings to find their way in a tangled world.

THE CRUCIAL ISSUE: DOES TRADITIONAL AMERICAN PUBLIC EDUCATION HAVE A FUTURE?

Roderick R. Paige, the U.S. secretary of education, said in a speech to the National Association of Elementary School Principals that "public schools are the greatest social invention in the history of America. You and I must protect them and make them strong."[11] He explained that excellent public schools achieve more than the academic goal of helping all children reach high standards. They also shape a common culture shared by the general public. "Public schools not only serve the public," he said. "They create the public." They create a public, Paige insisted, that values democracy. To make this point, he cited the familiar saying, "Teachers are the real heroes of democracy. Others may defend it, but teachers create it."

Secretary Paige apparently believes that teaching young people democracy and helping them achieve academic excellence are the central aims of education and that these aims can be achieved by individual teachers and principals working in their respective schools. Schools will improve, he said, "as a result of what happens because of the men and women who walk down the halls of our schools and look into the eyes of the children. They are the ones who will make the difference."

The people in a school's halls are most likely to teach young people to value democratic principles if they work in traditional public schools that bring together young people from a variety of races, ethnic groups, and social-economic conditions. These public schools provide a context for understanding democracy. As an elementary school principal from Fairfax County, Virginia, said, "The children in my school come from all over the world, from places like Bolivia, San Salvador, Ecuador, Ethiopia, Romania, and Russia. They speak forty-four different languages. To these kids, the world is not a scary place because they learn surrounded by friends from different countries and races, and this experience shows them that everyone is basically the same."[12] An evenhanded, single system of education that invites a diversity of students to appreciate their common humanity gives young people a deeply felt understanding of the principle of equality that sustains any democracy. This principle cannot be taught by a system that segregates children or by an individual teacher trapped in a segregated world.

Unfortunately, segregation seems to be increasing in the twenty-first century. Jonathan Kozol's *Savage Inequalities* describes the "filth and despair" that abound in "death zones," a term for ghetto neighborhoods, where schools typically lack textbooks, magazines, chalk, and VCRs and desks are antiquated, biology labs have no laboratory tables, and many rooms have no heat in winter.[13] Students attending these schools realize that white children living in the suburbs attend clean, cheerful schools. The inequity is not lost on them. As one teacher in a ghetto elementary school, Public School 261 in District 10, said to Kozol, "All these children see TV. . . . They know what suburban schools are like. Then they look around them at their school. This was a roller-rink, you know. . . . They understand."[14]

THINKING IN NEW WAYS TO SAVE EDUCATION AND DEMOCRACY

To achieve Secretary Paige's admirable vision of schools that teach students to live democratically and to reach high academic standards, we must change our thinking. Parents, public officials, business leaders, and educators must discard thinking that justifies the existence of derelict public schools. They must reject thinking that justifies developing independent publicly financed schools, charter schools, if these have the effect of segregating children. They must also resist charter schools whose implicit agenda is to inculcate in young people unthinking acceptance of circumscribed, unexamined convictions. Schools that eschew critical thinking and thwart equality of opportunity threaten democracy. Democracy requires that schools teach children to think well, precisely, honestly, and objectively about complex issues. Democracy requires that schools train children to be open-minded and willing to change their minds in the face of new evidence. Democracy requires that schools educate students to respect and support those of various races, ethnicities, and genders. It requires thinking in fresh, new ways that see schools as natural systems in a universe of natural systems.[15]

American education is in danger of being dismantled. To preserve it requires adopting a new way of thinking about educating young people.

Modern science says that all living systems are interrelated and that human beings are connected to one other and to everything, living and nonliving, on Earth. Let us think, then, in a new way about interrelatedness in our schools. Let us build strong relationships among those working and learning in schools and firm bonds between school and community. Let us prepare young people to live democratically and compassionately in a seething and violent world by instilling in them the unwavering knowledge that they, too, are inextricably joined to all human beings.

Modern science says that everything self-organizes in response to its environment. Think, then, in a new way about the learning environment we give our children. Human beings self-organize. That is, they adapt to their environment. If they occupy barren, dark places, then they may develop barren souls suited to darkness. If young people attend filthy, crumbling, stench-filled schools, then they may develop minds of rage and desolation. If young people occupy gleaming, pristine, homogeneous worlds where everyone resembles them, then their souls may grow small and impervious to light.

Modern science says that we live on a planet filled with differentiation. Earth churns with creativity, generating infinite diversity. Think, then, in a new way about the beauty and wonder of the diversity around us, seen in the ocean's waves, in different races and cultures, and in the uniqueness of every voice. In America's schools let us weave diversity into an elegant whole tapestry where everyone contributes, everyone is related to everyone else, and the whole is decidedly different from and far more wonderful than the sum of its parts.

If we intentionally relate to others, if we maintain a learning environment that nurtures self-organizing human beings, if we cherish the beauty and variety of our diverse world, then surely Americans can revive and sustain a single system of public education that is worthy of their children. Surely in such a system, the two fundamental aims of education can be achieved. Students will reach high academic standards as they learn, understand, and think deeply about difficult academic subjects, and they will discover that life *is* relationships. Humanity is indivisible, and all life on Earth is indivisible, too.

NOTES

1. The material on mathematics is drawn from Judy Reihard, "Contextual Teaching and Learning of Mathematics," unpublished MS, 2003; as well as from her presentations at conferences in Anchorage, Alaska, and Billings, Montana. A vocational mathematics specialist, Reihard helps teachers across the curriculum in the Tempe Union High School District incorporate mathematics into their respective subject areas. Before becoming a district mathematics specialist, Reihard was a classroom teacher for thirty-five years. On three occasions she received the Award of Excellence for her ability to make mathematics accessible to students of all ages and abilities. Reihard is currently in demand throughout the nation for her expert ability to teach mathematics in the context of students' lives. Her website, www.evtpc.org/tutor, provides resources for teaching mathematics in context.

2. Jerry Pallotta, *Hershey's Milk Chocolate Bar Fractions Book* (New York: Scholastic Inc., 1999), cited in Reihard, "Contextual Teaching and Learning of Mathematics," 4.

3. Tony Occhiuzzi of Tempe High School, Tempe, Ariz., and Dan Zavaleta of Desert Vista High School, Phoenix, Ariz., deserve special praise for their hand in connecting algebra, geometry, and trigonometry to building solar-powered boats.

4. Bernard Jones of McClintock High School, Tempe, Ariz., inspires interest in, and high standards for, the geography project.

5. Tina H. Straley and Robert W. Hill, "Partnerships at Dartmouth: Mathematics, Art, and the Humanities," *Focus: The Newsletter of the Mathematical Association of America* (1999), available at www.dartmouth.edu/~matc (accessed 9 September 2002).

6. Lt. Col. Dave Grossman, "Teaching Kids to Kill," in Lynne Oldfield, *Free to Learn* (Gloucestershire, England: Hawthorn Press, 2001), 105.

7. David Perkins, *Smart Schools: Better Thinking and Learning for Every Child* (New York: Free Press, 1992), 31.

8. Lawrence A. Cremin, *American Education: The Metropolitan Experience, 1876–1980* (New York: Harper and Row, 1988), 415.

9. Ellen J. Langer, *The Power of Mindful Learning* (Cambridge, Mass.: Perseus Books, 1997), 111.

10. Langer, *The Power of Mindful Learning,* 137, 75.

11. Roderick R. Paige, keynote presentation, National Association of Elementary School Principals Conference, Anaheim, Calif., 12 April 2003. All

other references to Paige's views are also drawn from the notes I made of his keynote speech.

12. Mary Ann Ryan, National Association of Elementary School Principals Conference, Anaheim, Calif., April 2003. Ryan, who had served for many years as an elementary school principal in Virginia, described the challenges and advantages of working with a diverse student population.

13. Jonathan Kozol, *Savage Inequalities: Children in America's Schools* (New York: HarperPerennial, 1992), 5.

14. Kozol, *Savage Inequalities,* 88.

15. For a cogent analysis of the destructive force of business on education and a call for new thinking about public education, see Michael Engel, *The Struggle for Control of Public Education* (Philadelphia: Temple University Press, 2000), 68–89.

Bibliography

Allen, Rick. "Big Schools: The Way We Are." *Educational Leadership* 59, no. 5 (February 2002): 36–41.

American Association for the Advancement of Science. *The Liberal Art of Science: Agenda for Action.* Washington, D.C.: American Association for the Advancement of Science, 1990.

American Council on the Teaching of Foreign Languages. *National Standards for Foreign Language Education.* New York: American Council on the Teaching of Foreign Languages, 1999.

Anderson, James D. "Introduction" to "Why Don't You Go to School with Us?" In Sheila Curran Bernard and Sarah Mondale, *School: The Story of American Public Education,* ed. Sarah Mondale and Sarah B. Patton, 123–30. Boston: Beacon Press, 2001.

Annan, Kofi. "Nobel Lecture December 10, 2001." *Timeline,* no. 63 (May–June 2002): 6–9.

Ark, Tom Vander. "The Case for Small High Schools." *Educational Leadership* 59, no. 5 (February 2002): 55–59.

Bateson, Gregory. *Mind and Nature: A Necessary Unity.* New York: Bantam Books, 1990.

Bernard, Sheila Curran, and Sarah Mondale. *School: The Story of American Public Education.* Ed. Sarah Mondale and Sarah B. Patton. Boston: Beacon Press, 2001.

Berry, Thomas. *The Great Work: Our Way into the Future.* New York: Bell Tower, 1999.

Biddle, Bruce J., and David C. Berliner. "Small Class Size and Its Effects." *Educational Leadership* 59, no. 5 (February 2002): 12–23.

Brown, Molly, and Joanna Macy. "Teaching Sustainability: Whole Systems Learning." Unpublished MS, 11 October 2002.

Capra, Frijof. *The Turning Point: Science, Society, and the Rising Culture.* New York: Bantam Books, 1988.

————. *The Web of Life: A New Scientific Understanding of Living Systems.* New York: Anchor, 1996.

Carter, Gene. "Watching Out for Our Poorest Schools." Available at www. ascd.org/educationnews/kids/kids092002.html (accessed 15 March 2002).

Chaisson, Eric J. *Cosmic Evolution: The Rise of Complexity in Nature.* Cambridge: Harvard University Press, 2001.

Chubb, John E., and Terry M. Moe. *Politics, Markets, and America's Schools.* Washington, D.C.: Brookings Institution, 1990.

Colebrook, Michael. "The New Universe Story." Available at www.greenspirit.org.uk (accessed 3 April 2003).

Cremin, Lawrence A. *American Education: The Metropolitan Experience, 1876–1980.* New York: Harper and Row, 1988.

Cuban, Larry. "Introduction" to "A Nation at Risk?" In Sheila Curran Bernard and Sarah Mondale, *School: The Story of American Public Education.* Ed. Sarah Mondale and Sarah B. Patton, 173–82. Boston: Beacon Press, 2001.

Deming, W. Edwards. *The New Economics.* Cambridge: MIT Center for Advance Engineering Study, 1994.

Donovan, M. Suzanne, John D. Bransford, and James Peggegrino, eds. *How People Learn: Bridging Research and Practice.* Washington, D.C.: National Academy Press, 1999.

Douglas, William O. *The Bible and the Schools.* Boston: Little, Brown, 1966.

Duncan, Todd L. "Contextual Teaching and Learning of Science." Unpublished MS, 2003.

————. "Guidance from Nature." Unpublished MS, 19 March 2003.

————. *An Ordinary World: The Role of Science in Your Search for Personal Meaning.* Hillsboro, Oreg.: Science Integration Institute, 2001.

Ellis, Joseph. *Founding Brothers: The Revolutionary Generation.* New York: Vintage Books, 2000.

Elmore, Richard F. "Testing Trap: The Single Largest—and Possibly Most Destructive—Federal Intrusion into America's Public Schools." *Harvard Magazine,* September–October 2002: 35–37, 97.

Engel, Michael. *The Struggle for Control of Public Education.* Philadelphia: Temple University Press, 2000.

Finn, Chester E., Jr., Bruno V. Manno, and Gregg Vanourek. *Charter Schools in Action: Renewing Public Education.* Princeton: Princeton University Press, 2000.

Finser, Torin M. *School Renewal: A Spiritual Journey for Change.* Great Barrington, Mass.: Anthroposophic Press, 2001.

Fraser, James W. *Between Church and State: Religion and Public Education in a Multicultural America.* New York: St. Martin's/Griffin, 1999.

Gardner, Howard. *Frames of Mind: The Theory of Multiple Intelligences,* 10th ed. New York: HarperCollins, 1993.

Gately, Gary. "Maryland: A Move for Smaller Schools." *The New York Times,* 10 October 2001: A2. Available at www.ruraledu.org/keep-learning.cfm? record-no+6141.

Greenfield, Susan. *The Human Brain: A Guided Tour.* New York: Harper-Collins, 1997.

Grossman, Lt. Col. Dave. "Teaching Kids to Kill." In Lynne Oldfield, *Free to Learn.* Gloucestershire, England: Hawthorn Press, 2001.

Gurney, David W. "Culture as the Context for Teaching Foreign Languages." Unpublished MS, 2003.

————. "Total Immersion of Welcome Outsiders: Cross-Cultural Encounters." In *A TESOL Professional Anthology.* Ed. Carol Cargill, 113–20. Lincolnwood, Ill.: Volunitad Publishers and National Textbook Co., 1987.

Hammonds, Keith H. "Size Is Not a Strategy." *Fast Company,* September 2002: 78–86.

Hobson, Art. *Physics: Concepts and Connections.* Englewood Cliffs, N.J.: Prentice-Hall, 1998.

Johnson, Elaine B. *Contextual Teaching and Learning: What It Is and Why It's Here to Stay.* Thousand Oaks, Calif.: Corwin Press, Inc., 2002.

Johnson, H. Thomas, and Anders Broms. *Profit beyond Measure: Extraordinary Results through Attention to Work and People.* New York: Free Press, 2000.

Kaestle, Carl F. "Introduction" to "The Educated Citizen." In Sheila Curran Bernard and Sarah Mondale, *School: The Story of American Public Education.* Ed. Sarah Mondale and Sarah B. Patton, 11–18. Boston: Beacon Press, 2001.

King, Martin Luther, Jr. "Where Do We Go from Here: Chaos or Community?" (1976). In *A Testament of Hope: The Essential Writing and Speeches of Martin Luther King, Jr.* Ed. James M. Washington, 555–633. San Francisco: HarperCollins, 1986.

Kohn, Alfie. *Beyond Discipline: From Compliance to Community.* Alexandria: Association for Supervision and Curriculum Development, 1996.

————. *The Case against Standardized Testing: Raising the Scores, Ruining the Schools.* Portsmouth, N.Y.: Heinemann, 2000.

Kozol, Jonathan. *Savage Inequalities: Children in America's Schools.* New York: HarperPerennial, 1992.

Kramsch, Claire. "Second Language Acquisition, Applied Linguistics, and the Teaching of Foreign Languages." *Modern Language Journal* 84, no. 3 (September 2000): 310–15.

Kronholz, June, and Robert S. Greenberger. "Supreme Court Ruling Gives Boost to Proponents of School Vouchers." *The Wall Street Journal,* 28 June 2002: A1, A4.

Langer, Ellen J. *The Power of Mindful Learning.* Cambridge, Mass.: Perseus Books, 1997.

Lazlo, Ervin. *The Systems View of the World.* New York: George Braziller, 1972.

Lincoln, Abraham. "Second Inaugural Address." Facsimile, Historical Documents Co., 1865.

Margulis, Lynn, and Dorian Sagan. *What Is Life?* New York: Simon and Schuster, 1995.

Mathews, David. *Is There a Public for Public Schools?* Dayton: Kettering Foundation Press, 1996.

Maturana, Humberto, and Pille Bunnell. "The Biology of Business: Love Expands Intelligence." *Reflections: The SoL Journal* 1, no. 2 (winter 1999): 58–62.

———. "Biosphere, Homosphere, and Robosphere: What Has That to Do with Business?" Available at www.sol-ne.org/res/wp/maturana (accessed January 1999) (based on a presentation made by Humberto Maturana to the Society for Organizational Learning Members' Meeting, Amherst, Mass., June 1998).

Meadows, Donella. "Economics Laws Clash with the Planet's." *Timeline,* no. 57 (May–June 2001): 8–9.

Menand, Louis. *The Metaphysical Club: A Story of Ideas in America.* New York: Farrar, Straus and Giroux, 2001.

Miron, Gary, and Christopher Nelson. *What's Public about Charter Schools? Lessons Learned about Choice and Accountability.* Thousand Oaks, Calif.: Corwin Press, Inc., 2002.

National Research Council. *National Science Education Standards.* Washington, D.C.: National Academy Press, 1996.

NCCSR Bookmark 3, no. 9 (September 2002). Available at www.goodschools.gwu.edu/pubs/book/sep02.html (accessed 10 March 2002).

Omaggio-Handley, Alice. *Teaching Language in Context.* Boston: Heinle and Heinle, 1986.

Paige, Roderick R. Keynote presentation, National Association of Elementary School Principals Conference, Anaheim, Calif., 12 April 2003.

Pallotta, Jerry. *Hershey's Milk Chocolate Bar Fractions Book.* New York: Scholastic Inc., 1999.

Perkins, David. *Smart Schools: Better Thinking and Learning for Every Child.* New York: Free Press, 1992.

Phillips, June K., and Robert M. Terry, eds. *Foreign Language Standards:*

Linking Research, Theories, and Practices. Lincolnwood, Ill.: National Textbook Co. and American Council on the Teaching of Foreign Languages, 1999.

Popham, W. James. *The Truth about Testing: An Educator's Call to Action.* Alexandria: Association for Supervision and Curriculum Development, 2001.

Ravitch, Diane. "Introduction" to "You Are an American." In Sheila Curran Bernard and Sarah Mondale, *School: The Story of American Public Education.* Ed. Sarah Mondale and Sarah B. Patton. Boston: Beacon Press, 2001.

———. *Left Back: A Century of Battles over School Reform.* New York: Simon and Schuster, 2000.

Reihard, Judy. "Contextual Teaching and Learning of Mathematics." Unpublished MS, 2003. Available at www.ruraledu.org/keep-learning.cfm?record-no+614.

Restak, Richard. *The Secret Life of the Brain.* New York: Dana Press and Joseph Henry Press, 2002.

Rivers, Wilga. *A Practical Guide to the Teaching of French.* Lincolnwood, Ill.: National Textbook Co., 1968.

Rothstein, Richard. "A School District Refuses to Worship Scores Alone." *The New York Times,* 14 February 2002: A23.

———. "The Growing Revolt against the Tester." *The New York Times,* 30 May 2001: A2.

Ryan, Mary Ann. National Association of Elementary School Principals Conference, Anaheim, Calif., April 2003.

Savage, David G. "Court Upholds School Vouchers." *The Oregonian,* 28 June 2002: A1, A15.

Senge, Peter. "View from the Chair." *Reflections* 4, no. 2 (winter 2002): 78–79.

Siegel, Jessica. "The Community Scholar: Pedro Antonio Noguera Is a 'Pragmatic Optimist' about Urban Schools." *Harvard Magazine,* January–February 2002: 50–54.

Smolin, Lee. *The Life of the Cosmos.* New York: Widenfeld and Nicolson, 1997.

Spear, Lorna. "Improving Bemiss Elementary School." Presented at the Washington State School Improvement Conference, Tacoma, 5 November 2002.

Spring, Joel. *The American School: 1642–2000,* 5th ed. Boston: McGraw-Hill, 2000.

Starr, Alexandra. "Why Johnny Can't Fail." *Business Week,* 25 November 2002: 72–74.

Sternberg, Robert J. "Teaching Wisdom in Our Schools." *Education Week on the Web,* 13 November 2002. Available at http://ew/ewstory.cfm?slug=//Sternberg.h22#author (accessed 15 November 2002).

Straley, Tina H., and Robert W. Hill. "Partnerships at Dartmouth: Mathematics, Art, and the Humanities." *Focus: The Newsletter of the Mathematical Association of America* (1999). Available at www.dartmouth.edu/~matc (accessed 9 September 2002).

Swimme, Brian. *The Hidden Heart of the Cosmos: Humanity and the New Story.* Maryknoll, N.Y.: Orbis Books, 1999.

————. *The Universe Is a Green Dragon: A Cosmic Creation Story.* Santa Fe: Bear and Co. Publishing, 1984.

————, performer. *The Fundamental Order of the Cosmos.* Mill Valley, Calif.: New Story Project Video, 1990 (video).

Swimme, Brian, and Thomas Berry. *The Universe Story: From the Primordial Flaring Forth to the Ecozoic Era.* San Francisco: HarperSanFrancisco, 1992.

Symonds, William C. "Closing the School Gap: If No Child Is to Be Left Behind, We Must Overhaul Funding." *Business Week,* 14 October 2002: 124–25.

Tyack, David. "Introduction." In Sheila Curran Bernard and Sarah Mondale, *School: The Story of American Public Education.* Ed. Sarah Mondale and Sarah B. Patton, 1–8. Boston: Beacon Press, 2001.

Wasley, Patricia A. "Small Classes, Small Schools: The Time Is Now." *Educational Leadership* 59, no. 5 (February 2002): 6–10.

Wheatley, Margaret J. *Leadership and the New Science.* San Francisco: Berrett-Koehler Publishers, 1992.

Wheeler, John A. "Information, Physics, Quantum: The Search for Links." In *Complexity, Entropy and the Physics of Information.* Ed. Wojciech H. Zurek. Cambridge, Mass.: Perseus Publishing, 1990.

Wheeler, John A., K. S. Thorne, and C. Misner. *Gravitation.* San Francisco: Freeman, 1973.

Whitehead, Alfred North. "The Aims of Education." In *Aims of Education and Other Essays.* New York: Macmillan Co., 1929.

Wills, Garry. "Lincoln's Greatest Speech?" *Atlantic Monthly,* September 1999: 60–70.

Wyatt, Edward. "Higher Scores Aren't Cure-All, School Run for Profit Learns." *The New York Times,* 13 March 2001: A1–A2.

Yeats, William Butler. "Among School Children." In *The Collected Poems of W. B. Yeats.* New York: Macmillan Publishing Co., 1956.

Zukav, Gary. *The Dancing Wu Li Masters: An Overview of the New Physics.* New York: William Morrow, 1979.

Index

Abbott, Edwin Abbott, 116
Abington v. Schempp, 9
academic goals of education, ix, 1
academic standards: of charter
    schools, 32–33; in vocational
    education, 14–16
accountability: in business model,
    24–25; and public education,
    35–44
Annan, Kofi, 16
art, mathematics and, 117–18
assessment: alternative, 37;
    continuous, 84–85, *85;* reform of,
    42; standardized tests, 35–44
awareness, in universe, 61

Babbitt, Natalie, 116
Bateson, Gregory, 92
Bemiss Elementary School:
    assessment at, *85;* reform at,
    72–75, 80
bilingual instruction, 74
Black, Hugo, 6
Brookings Institute, 33
Brown, Margaret Wise, 115
Brown v. Board of Education, 4
Buber, Martin, 8–9

bullying, xi
bureaucratization of public education,
    xi; elimination of, 49n27
business: and schools, 45–46; and
    vocational education, 12–16
business model: effects of, 25–26;
    elements of, 22–25; and public
    education, xiii–xiv, 21–51

Catholic schools, 7–8
charter schools, xi–xii, xii–xiii,
    28–35; evaluation of, 32–33;
    nature of, 28–32; and social
    change, 33–35
Chubb, John E., xi
Coalition for Essential Schools, 35
coercion: in democracy, xi;
    religious, 10
collaboration: and educational
    reform, 72–75; leadership and, 77
common culture, 1–2, 16–17;
    vouchers and, 7–8
community, and educational reform,
    80–81
competition: in business model,
    23–24; and public education,
    28–35

Conant, James B., 26
connections, making, leadership
and, 76
Constitutional Rights Foundation, 1
contextual teaching, 89–103;
definition of, 92; elements of, 95;
in history, 90–92; principles of
modern science and, 91–95; for
subject learning, 95–100; in
vocational education, 14–16
creativity, leadership and, 79
Cremin, Lawrence A., 1, 119
criterion-referenced tests, 39
critical thinking, 118–19; leadership
and, 78
Cuban, Larry, 21

Darwin, Charles, 23
Deming, W. Edwards, 24
democracy, 5; and charter schools,
31; and common culture, 2;
criticisms of, xi; educational
reform and, 121–22
detail, attention to, leadership and, 77
Dewey, John, 5
differentiation, xiv, 10–11, 63–65;
and context, 94–95; and
education, 65; and leadership,
79–80
disadvantaged populations: IQ tests
and, 13; slavery and, 3–4
diversity, 4–5, 120; avoidance of,
5–6; and foreign language
learning, 98–99; increase in, 2;
leadership and, 79; religious,
appreciation of, 11; teaching
respect for, ix–x
Douglas, William O., 10
Duncan, Todd, 96, 102n8

EAI. *See* Educational Alternatives
Inc.
Edison Schools, Inc., 30, 45
educated person, defining, 105–6
Educational Alternatives Inc. (EAI),
45–46
educational management
organizations (EMOs), 45–46
educational reform, xiii, 69–88; in
1980s and 1990s, x; approaches
to, 121–22; of assessment, 42;
controversy over, 21; success in,
72–75
Elmore, Richard F., 69
EMOs. *See* educational management
organizations
Engle v. Vitale, 9
equal opportunity: contextual
teaching and, 100–101; lack of,
2–6, 34, 121; mathematics
instruction and, 106; vocational-
technical education and, 16;
vouchers and, 6–8

Finn, Chester E., 30, 46
foreign language learning,
contextual, 98–100, 102n9
founders: and educational system,
3–4; and separation of church and
state, 9
Franklin, Benjamin, 3
Fraser, James W., 8–9
freedom of religion, 9–10
funding of education: and reform,
70–72; and vouchers, 6–7

Gates, Henry Louis, Jr., 2
goals of education, 1–19; academic,
ix, 1; social, ix–x, 1, 7–8, 16–17

growth: in business model, 22–23; and public education, 26–28

Gurney, David, 96, 99

Hamburger Rubric, *85*
history, contextual teaching in, 90–92
home schooling, xii
Home Visit Project, 80–81
hope, leadership and, 78–79
humanity, indivisibility of, ix, 16, 120

immigration, 4, 13
innovation, xiii; charter schools and, 28–29
interest groups, educational goals of, 1
interrelatedness, xiv, 10, 58–60; and assessment, 36; in business, 25; and charter schools, xiii; and common culture, 2; and context, 92–93; and education, 59–60; and leadership, 76–77; in quantum worldview, 57
IQ tests, 13

Jackson, Robert, 10

Kaestle, Carl, 31
Kehrberg, Kirk D., 90–92, 101n1
King, Martin Luther, Jr., 4
Kohn, Alfie, 44
Kozol, Jonathan, 34, 121

language learning, contextual, 98–100, 102n9
leadership: and differentiation, 79–80; and interdependence,

76–77; principles of modern science and, 75–80; and self-organization, 77–79
Lincoln, Abraham, 3–4
literature, mathematics and, *115,* 115–16
local control, of charter schools, 31–32

manipulatives, for mathematics instruction, 106–11, *107–9, 111*
Mann, Horace, 8
maps, painting, 113, *114*
Margulis, Lynn, 61
market: and charter schools, xii; and competition, 23
mathematics teaching: contextual, 105–24; strategies for, 106–18
Maturana, Humberto, 62, 93
McClintock High School, 113, *114*
Miron, Gary, 34
Moe, Terry M., xi
movement, and abstract ideas, 112, *113*
music, mathematics and, 116–17, *117*

National Education Association, Commission on the Reorganization of Secondary Education, 12–13
natural selection, 23
Nelson, Christopher, 34
Newtonian worldview, 54–55
No Child Left Behind Act, 36, 38
norm-referenced tests, 38–39

Orfield, Gary, 2

Paige, Roderick R., 120
parents: and charter schools, 31; and educational reform, 80–81; and standardized testing, 43–44
participation, in quantum worldview, 57
Perkins, David, 119
physical movement, and abstract ideas, 112, *113*
Popham, W. James, 41
principals, 75–76
process, attention to, leadership and, 77
products, mathematics instruction and, 112–14, *114*
Protestantism, 1, 8–10
public education: business model and, 21–51; criticism of, x–xi; differentiation and, 65; dismantling of, ix–xv; in 1980s, x; establishment of, 2–3; future of, 120–21; importance of, ix; interdependence and, 59–60; principles of modern science and, 53–67; religion and, 8–11; self-organization and, 62–63; term, 47

quantum worldview, 55–59

racism, 3–4
Rehnquist, William, 6
Reihard, Judith, 96, 123n1
religion, in public schools, 8–11
religious freedom, 9–10
respect, teaching, ix–x, 5; leadership and, 78
results-based management: in business model, 24–25; and public education, 35–44
Ryan, Mary Ann, 120, 124n12

school size, 26–28
science, modern, principles of, xiv; and contextual teaching, 91–95; and educational reform, 122; and leadership, 75–80; and public education, 53–67; and religion in education, 10–11; and school size, 28
science teaching, contextual, 96–98, 102n8
segregation, 3–4, 34
self-organization, xiv, 10, 60–63; and context, 93–94; and education, 62–63; and leadership, 77–79
separation of church and state, 6, 9
Sharp, Carol, 81
slavery, 3–4
Smolin, Lee, 91
social change, charter schools and, 33–35
social goals of education, ix–x, 1, 16–17; vouchers and, 7–8
social problems, schools and, xi
sorting, 7; charter schools and, 34; IQ tests and, 13–14
Souter, David, 6
Spear, Lorna L., 74–76
Spencer, Herbert, 23
standardized tests, 35–44; effects on children, 41–42
Sternberg, Robert J., 1
superintendents, 75
Susan B. Anthony Elementary School, 80–81

target setting: in business model, 24–25; and public education, 35–44
teachers: criticism of, 82; and educational reform, 81–85

teaching. *See* contextual teaching
television, influence of, 118–19
thinking. *See* critical thinking
tracking, 13–14
traditional public school system:
future of, 120–21; and teaching
respect for diversity, 5; term, xii.
See also public education
transparency, in charter schools,
30
Tyack, David, 83

violence: in schools, xi; television
viewing and, 119

vocational education: 1880–1917,
12–14; 1980–present, 14–16
voucher programs, xii, 6–8

Washington, George, 3
Welch, Jack, 25
Wheeler, John, 55–56
women, education of, 13
worldviews, 28, 53; Newtonian,
54–55; quantum, 55–59

Yeats, William Butler, 57

Zukav, Gary, 59

About the Author

Dr. Elaine B. Johnson, the executive director of MBM Associates, consultants to educators and business leaders, was for many years a tenured university professor and administrator, a dean of community college vocational and academic programs, and a high school teacher and department chair. A prominent figure in the reform of education, Johnson has done extensive research, writing, and speaking on the influence of brain research on teaching and learning. She connects brain research to the classroom in her book *Contextual Teaching and Learning: What It Is and Why It's Here to Stay* (2002). Johnson is also coauthor of a series of four literature textbooks for grades nine–twelve entitled Literature for Life and Work (1997). This series invites students to discover meaning in literature by placing it in the context of their daily lives and experiences. A Woodrow Wilson fellow, Johnson has received numerous awards for her work as an educator.

Endorsements

"Can quantitative measurement—a basic tenant of the business model—by itself be the only measure of success? Applied to education, does this model ignore the value of relationships? These questions form the core of today's education debate. Dr. Johnson challenges us to look to the universal principles of modern science at work in all-natural systems to restore our confidence in public education. *The Dismantling of Public Education and How to Stop It* is a courageous, provocative, well-researched book that frames and takes a stand on the debate whose outcome affects us all."—Arlene H. Parisot, Office of the Commissioner of Higher Education, Montana University System

"Elaine Johnson has the courage to suggest the business model fails public education and touts a contextual science model as a dynamic systemic change agent for success. The idea of making connections is a sound concept when applied to the teaching of mathematics. Experiences children can relate to connect mathematical concepts to a deeper level of understanding than rote memorization can achieve. This book challenges the entire teaching community to engage students in solving significant problems to allow them to experience meaning and acquire understanding and knowledge."—Jill Sumerlin, recipient of the 2000 Presidential Award for Excellence in Mathematics and Science Teaching

"The title grabs attention in its suggestion of a disassembling of public education in the United States. Dr. Johnson expertly presents the case. However, she is most admirable in her discussion of means to correct or rebuild the structure of our educational system. I see the embedded theme as the power of the group, or in today's vernacular, the learning community. Time, experience, and research have proven the value of multilevel, multidirectional team effort in the identification and resolution of difficult situations. Dr. Johnson has masterfully illuminated the process." —Gloria Heberley, Temple University